Discovering John

THE GOSPEL ACCORDING TO JOHN

Discovering John Myron Augsburger
What This Scripture Means to Me Dorothy Shellenberger
Photographs Bruce C. Cresson
Maps Janice Gibson
Book Design Elizabeth Woll
Cover Artist Ben Wolhberg

DISCOVERING JOHN

The Guideposts Home Bible Study Program

GUIDEPOSTS

Carmel   New York 10512

THE GUIDEPOSTS HOME BIBLE STUDY PROGRAM
The Gospel According to John:
    1. DISCOVERING JOHN
    2. My Working Bible
    3. My Journal of John
    4. Knowing More About John

Contents

How to Use the Guideposts Home Bible Study Program

Step #1: Open your Working Bible. Read the passages corresponding to Lesson 1 in your hardcover text and make notes.

Step #2: Then study Lesson 1 in the hardcover text. Go back and add any questions or comments in the spaces provided in the Working Bible. Keep your Working Bible open so you can look up the many Scripture references in the lesson.

Step #3: Turn to your check-yourself booklet. Try out the self-testing puzzles, quizzes and exercises designed to make your home study program fun. Repeat this "rhythm" of study for Lessons 2 through 8.

Step #4: Open your pocket journal. Read the Scripture verses and use the special prayers to include your Bible study in your daily devotionals. Remember to carry the journal around with you to write your personal reflections.

Publisher's Introduction

"John, perceiving that what had reference to the bodily things of Jesus' ministry had been sufficiently related, and encouraged by his friends, and inspired by the Holy Spirit, wrote a spiritual gospel."

This perceptive comment written in the third century by Clement of Alexandria, one of the most profound scholars in the early church, will most certainly come alive for us as we study the Gospel of John. For countless millions of Christians, this "spiritual Gospel" has been, and is, the most loved book in our Bible.

In our study of the synoptic Gospels—Matthew, Mark, and Luke—we saw clearly that none of these writers attempted to record a biographical or historical account of Jesus' life and ministry. This is equally true, if not more so, of this fourth Gospel. And while there are similarities between this Gospel and the other three, there are also significant differences.

For example, the Gospel of John does not include the stories about the birth of Jesus. We find nothing here about His baptism or His confrontation with Satan in the wilderness. Missing also are the lively and graphic parables that are found in the other Gospels. And there is no mention of the moving account of Jesus' final meal with His disciples in the upper room on the night before His crucifixion.

But the Gospel of John fills out the story of Jesus by

including certain episodes and teachings not found in the other three: the wedding at Cana; the conversation between Nicodemus and Jesus which gives us the gospel in a nutshell (3:16); the meeting at Jacob's well between Jesus and the woman of Sychar in Samaria; the return of Lazarus from the dead at Jesus' command; and the marvelous servant-teaching of Jesus when He washed the feet of His disciples after what we have come to know as the Last Supper.

Peculiar also to the Gospel of John are the seven "I am" statements of Jesus: I am the bread of life; I am the light of the world; I am the door; I am the good shepherd; I am the resurrection and the life; I am the way, the truth, and the life; I am the true vine.

It is clear that the writer of this Gospel was intimately familiar with not only Jesus' words but His thoughts. As in no other place we sense the thinking and the heart of Jesus as John pulls aside the curtain and helps us come to grips with His meaning.

The early church passed along the tradition that this Gospel was written at Ephesus by the Apostle John toward the end of his life, possibly between 70 and 100 A.D. However, there are those who date it much earlier. Also there are those who express uncertainty as to whether all of the Gospel actually came from John's pen. But it seems certain that it originated from the heart and reflections of the Apostle John himself.

In our study so far we have moved in the footsteps of Jesus up and down Palestine, we have listened to His words, and have stood in awe at His actions as related in *Matthew*, *Mark*, and *Luke*. Now, as we move through the pages of the Gospel of John all of this combines to give us all that we can understand about Jesus the Messiah, the Christ, the eternal Son of God—the central Figure of all four Gospels and of history.

Preface

The Gospel of John may well be regarded as the most universal of the four Gospels. According to its own claims, it was written that we might believe "that Jesus is the Christ, the Son of God, and that believing ye might have life through his name" (20:31).

John's Gospel was probably written at Ephesus by the beloved disciple and his assistants. Irenaeus, the Bishop of Lyons, c. 180, who had known the aged Polycarp, a convert and colleague of John, wrote, "John, the disciple of the Lord, who leaned on his breast, himself issued the Gospel while dwelling in Ephesus."

The Gospel may have been written as early as A.D. 80 or even before. We know it was being circulated in Egypt by A.D. 130 because of a papyrus fragment of the Gospel that was found there in 1920. Allowing a generation for it to travel means that the Gospel was written at least by A.D. 100—a time close enough to the events in the earthly life of Jesus to assure the book's historical accuracy, and far enough removed to avoid emotional embellishments.

John's Gospel is unique in comparison with the other three Gospels, which are known as the Synoptics. John selected materials from the life and teachings of Jesus to develop for his Greek readers a presentation of Christ as God's Son and the Saviour of the world. While not written chronologically, which seems to be more the case in the Synoptics, this Gospel, like the others, is basically telling the Jesus story. John does not chronicle some of the stories found in the Synoptics, such as Jesus' baptism, temptation, transfiguration, institution of the Lord's Supper, and agony in the Garden. He does, however, relate a number of additional accounts, such as Jesus' dialogue with Nicodemus, His meeting with the Samaritan woman, the raising of Lazarus, the foot-washing, the trial before Annas, and several post-resurrection appearances. John's primary divergence is in arrangement, for example, placing the cleansing of the temple at the beginning of Jesus' ministry, probably a choice to achieve John's purposes in composition.

John's theological approach begins with the pre-existent Christ being incarnate in Jesus of Nazareth. He treats Jesus' miracles as "signs," identifying Him as the Son of God. He presents the "King" rather than the Kingdom. While in the Synoptics the "kingdom of God" is a common theme, in John's Gospel the Kingdom is interpreted in terms of the larger theme of fellowship with God (3:3–5; 18:36). John writes of the new life which Christ came to bring us. And this life is presented as a faith relationship with the Father through Christ, mediated to us by the Spirit of God (Ch. 3, 6, 10, 15, 16, 17).

Reading Matthew 11:27 we are impressed that John's theology is not other than that heard by the other disciples. In Matthew Jesus says, "All things are delivered unto me of my Father; and no man knoweth the Son, but the Father; neither knoweth any man the Father, save the Son, and he to whomsoever the Son will reveal him." Similarly John writes, "No man hath seen God at any time; the only begotten Son, which is in the bosom of the Father, he hath declared him" (1:18). This is an important observation in view of the fact that nine-tenths of the material in John is not in the other Gospels.

Although certain scholars have debated the historical value of John's Gospel, more recent scholarship has come to see John's writing as perhaps a superior record of history. It is thought by some reliable interpreters that this Gospel reflects its Palestinian origin and is in some ways better than the other three.

John's Gospel is especially rich in identifying Jesus as the Son of God; in presenting the person of Jesus as the "I Am" of God (note the series of expressions, I Am the Bread of Life, I Am the Good Shepherd, I Am the Door, I Am the

True Vine, I Am the Way, the Truth, the Life); in discussing the Holy Spirit, with five great passages on His person and work; in sharing the upper-room discourses, including the marvelous high-priestly prayer; and in reviewing resurrection appearances to convince the skeptical disciples.

It has been said that John's Gospel is the earliest form of preaching the gospel—of telling the Jesus story. John holds the Jesus of history and the Christ of faith together as one and the same. John's Gospel interprets Jesus to Jew and gentile alike as the Redeemer who came to reconcile us to God. Christ is the One in whom God is manifested, "reconciling the world unto Himself" (2 Cor. 5:19).

John gave us this Gospel as a missionary tract, not as the gospel that Jesus taught but as the Gospel of Jesus Himself—He is the one who reconciles us to the Father. In some special way we have the fourth Gospel, as the Spirit's gift to His church, and it calls us to make Jesus the prescriptive, determining factor in our lives.

LESSON 1
JOHN 1–3

Christ the Reconciler— as the Word of Grace

Heavenly Father, Help me to hide Your Word in my heart that I might not sin against You. AMEN.

The message of grace is simply that "God was in Christ, reconciling the world unto himself" (2 Cor. 5:19). God took the initiative; He moved to us, overcoming our rebellion and estrangement by His love and reconciliation. In Jesus Christ we come to an understanding of God, and we come into fellowship with God (1:12). John writes, "For the law was given by Moses, but grace and truth came by Jesus Christ" (1:17). John introduces the reconciling work of Christ.

Jesus came "that we might have life, and have it more abundantly" (10:10). In His prayer He said, "And this is life eternal, that they might know thee, the only true God, and Jesus Christ whom thou hast sent" (17:3). In all of this we see that the Gospel of John was written to present Jesus as the eternal Son of God, the One in whom we know the Father, and in Whom we are reconciled to the Father. Jesus said, "I am the way, the truth, and the life, no man cometh to the Father but by me" (14:6).

John's Gospel opens with a poetic prologue (1:1–18) which is one of the most profound statements about Christ in Scripture. Here Jesus is presented as the eternal Logos (Word), who was with the Father from eternity—the beginning—and He identified with the Father as God.

The Word—as the Light of Life.

15

There are three affirmations made of the Word in this part of our Scripture lesson: First, "The Word was God" (1:1–2); second, the Word created all things (1:3–10); and third, the Word took human form and dwelled among us (1:11–18). This emphasis is spelled out graphically for us in Proverbs 8:22–31. You will find it helpful to turn to these verses and read them before continuing with this part of our study.

The mystery of the Incarnation is that God took human form to fully reveal Himself to us. Throughout the Old Testament, from stories of God's acts and discourses, we learn many profound things about Him. Now, in Jesus of Nazareth, this God of the Old Testament comes to us; we actually meet Him. Someone has well said that "either Jesus Christ was really God or we don't have a full revelation yet."

For God to become incarnate in human form without being sinful means that humanness and sinfulness are not synonymous (1:14). Instead, sinfulness is a perversion of humanness. From this we come to see that redemption is in some way the correction of the perversion; it is the re-creation of what is truly human! And since sinfulness is rebellion against God, salvation through Jesus Christ is our reconciliation to God, our becoming children of God. (1:11–12).

Martin Luther spoke of the three forms of the Word of God: 1) The eternal Word, the Christ; 2) the written Word, the Scripture; and 3) the preached Word, the witness in action. In the first eighteen verses of this Gospel all three forms are expressed. Jesus is the eternal Christ. John the Baptist is introduced as the prophetic witness (1:6–8). And the preaching of the word is expressed in the comments of John the Baptist (1:15) and of John the writer (1:16–18).

The concluding words of this prologue to the Gospel express the fact that the Living Word, the only begotten Son, came to make God known to us. We now have a God who is not an impersonal, abstract idea, but a God with a face. He is not "Someone out there"; He is here *with* us. In Jesus we can now address God as "Abba," as Father, or in a more familiar sense, He is "Daddy."

These first eighteen verses of the Gospel have been referred to by some as a possible hymn in the early Church. Whether this was so or not, the life of fellowship with God is a life of joy and celebration. Singing His praise is a meaningful part of our worship—an identification of believers

The Church of the Annunciation in Bethlehem with the statue of St. Jerome in the courtyard. In John 1:14 we read, "And the Word was made flesh, and dwelt among us." Here is celebrated both the birth of the Living Word and the importance of the written Word translated into the language of the people. Jerome is noted for his work of translating the Bible into the common Latin of his day.

with one another in the joy of reconciliation. And this reconciliation is in Jesus, the Word of God's grace. As John's introduction of his Gospel, these verses may be seen in three divisions: 1) the Word as the Incarnation (verses 1–2, 14); 2) the world and the Incarnation (verses 3–4, 10); and the witness to the Incarnation (verses 6–7, 15–17).

For us, to know Jesus is to know God, and to receive Jesus is to be reconciled to God. As Paul expressed this, "For he hath made him to be sin for us, who knew no sin; that we might be made the righteousness of God in him" (2 Cor. 5:21). In other words, the sinless Jesus assumed our sin so that we would be righteous in God's sight.

The Word—as the Lamb of God.

The story of Jesus is rooted in the acts of history. It is not a religious myth. It is the account of God's acts among people in Jesus Christ. For centuries, the Divine revelation—the Scriptures—had predicted the coming of the Christ.

Each of the four Gospels present John the Baptist, the wilderness preacher, as the herald of the King. John's message of repentance was more than a call to personal piety, it was a call for people to prepare for the coming of the Kingdom, for the arrival of the Messiah. His message was so clear and his ministry so successful that vast crowds of people were reached and moved. And the leaders of the Jewish religious bureaucracy came to inquire of John whether he was the Christ, the Messiah. This not only speaks of respect for John but tells us of the general expectation of the coming Messiah.

A study of John the Baptist as presented in the Gospels reveals his unique character. Yet Jesus said the lowliest person in the new Kingdom—His new fellowship—has greater privilege than had John. Of John himself we are shown that he had 1) a proper estimate of himself (1:19–26); 2) a spirit of humility (3:30); 3) a spiritual radiance (5:35); 4) a witness of righteousness (Mark 6:20); and 5) a clear witness of the Christ (10:41). In speaking of Jesus John said that he wasn't fit to unloose His sandals (1:27).

There are many names used to describe Jesus in John's Gospel, but one of the more expressive is this early statement from John the Baptist, "Behold the Lamb of God, who taketh away the sin of the world" (1:29). These words are reminiscent of Abraham's words to Isaac, "God will provide himself a lamb" (Gen. 22:8); and to the deliverance of Israel from Egypt with the sacrifice of the lamb for the

A picture of Cave 4 at Qumran. It was at Qumran in the Wilderness of Judea where the major biblical documents of the Dead Sea Scrolls were discovered in 1947. It was in this area where John the Baptist carried out his ministry.

passover (Ex. 12:1). They also remind us of Isaiah's words, "...he was brought as a lamb to the slaughter, and as a sheep before her shearers is dumb, so he opened not his mouth" (Isa. 53:7). Jesus is the lamb of God, "...our passover is sacrificed for us" (1 Cor. 5:7). In addition to the pictures of the Pascal (Passover) lamb and of the suffering servant, the Jewish community looked for an apocalyptic lamb in the final judgment.

It is clear that John in writing his Gospel is telling the

Jesus story with a theological interest. He is not simply giving a biography of the life of Christ, but he is lifting from the life of Jesus and arranging in his preferred order of illustration a selection of events and teachings that communicates the Good News of God's new fellowship. Having introduced Jesus as the eternal Word of God, he now presents Jesus as the atoning reconciler of people to God. The redemptive act of atonement is 1) to take away our sin; 2) to pay the price of forgiveness; and 3) to express the fullness of God's love.

The witness of John the Baptist presents Jesus as the one who fulfills God's promise as it was given through the Old Testamant prophets. John also bore witness to the Word from God that "Upon whom thou shalt see the Spirit descending and remaining on him, the same is he which baptizeth with the Holy Ghost" (1:33). John could therefore say, "This is the Son of God" (1:34). John's announcement is that above all, Jesus baptizes with the Spirit. He gives to His disciples of all time the gift of God's inner presence!

It is important to note that John described his own ministry as focused on Christ, saying that the sole purpose of his preaching and baptizing was that the Christ "should be made manifest," that is, that He should be made known to the people (1:31). And making Jesus known is the test of all true service. All that we do as witnesses, as worship leaders, as workers in social service, should point to Jesus.

Leonardo da Vinci, the early sixteenth-century artist, painted the Last Supper scene on a dining room wall in Milan. As a visitor stood viewing the finished work, he commented on the realism of several goblets on the table, exclaiming that they were so realistic he felt as though he could reach out and pick them up. Upon hearing those words the artist quickly grabbed a brush and painted out the goblets. Pointing to Jesus he said, "It's His face! His face, that I want you to see."

The Word—The Master.

We are now introduced to four men who became disciples of Jesus (1:35–51). A disciple is one who learns from and identifies with the Master. And the Christian life is discipleship of Jesus. A sixteenth-century Anabaptist, Hans Denck, said, "No one knows Christ truly unless he follows Him daily in life." Salvation is a relationship with Jesus, for in Him we are reconciled to God.

This part of our Scripture lesson is opened with a second affirmation by John that Jesus is the "Lamb of God" (1:29, 36). It was this identification of Jesus that led two of John the Baptist's disciples to leave him and follow Jesus. John always pointed attention away from himself to Jesus as the Messiah, the Christ.

In leaving John the Baptist and following Jesus these two men exhibited the supreme act of faith. Their attention was turned from the religion to which John had introduced them to the Person of Jesus whom they referred to as Master (1:38).

The directness of Jesus in His relationship with people is always interesting. When He realized the two men were following Him, He turned and asked what they wanted. They countered by asking where He lived—an indication that they wanted to be with Him. And in response Jesus said, "Come and see" (1:39). In reality this was an invitation not just to "see" or to talk, but to learn from Him. And their response was to follow Him and live with Him.

This is the essence of true discipleship—to be with Jesus. Their allegiance was transferred from John to Jesus. A faith that saves is faith in the Saviour, not faith in religion or in morality, but faith in Christ. As Paul wrote later, he had to discover that the righteousness of the law could only reconcile him with the law, but the righteousness of God in Christ reconciled him with God! (Phil. 3:9).

In this part of our lesson we see the Master as He walks into peoples' lives and calls them to be His disciples. And He does this today as He calls us to follow Him, to confess Him as Lord, and to become His servants.

One of the two disciples who turned to Jesus is identified as Andrew (1:40). Andrew, with the conviction that Jesus was actually the Christ, went first and found his brother Simon and brought him to Jesus (1:41–42). What a marvelous example we have in Andrew's first act of bringing his brother to Jesus. And in John's Gospel there are two other references to Andrew bringing people to Jesus: the lad with his lunch (6:8–9), and the Greeks who came to see Jesus (12:22). We need to join the fellowship of Andrew—bringing people to Jesus. This is our model today for witnessing. And we also need to recognize in this that salvation is not for individualistic piety but for community.

Some friends of ours moved into a new home. Across the field was an old house, and they were told that the old man who lived there was very inhospitable. Within a few days our friends baked a fresh apple pie and took it to his door with a friendly word. When the plate was returned later it contained an assortment of fresh fruit. From this beginning a relationship began to grow, and within a few months the neighbor accompanied my friends to church. In time, he made a personal commitment to Christ. All this happened because of an apple pie—and love.

When the Master makes disciples of people, it is not at a shallow level but with a full understanding of their person. In fact, His understanding of us enhances our own self-awareness. In our search for identity, Jesus, by His call, gives us our identity.

This truth is illustrated by Jesus' meeting with Simon when He gave him a new name. Jesus changed Simon's name to Cephas, which in Aramaic means "a rock"—Peter is the Greek translation of the same word. Jesus may well have given him the nickname "Rocky" as a prophecy of his future strength. Although it took Peter a while to realize his new identity, Jesus gave it to him at that moment. How wonderful it is that Jesus sees possibilities in us, as He did in Peter, that exceed anything we might imagine!

The scene now seems to shift from southern Palestine to the north in Galilee (1:43). Here, possibly in Cana, Jesus meets Philip whose home is in Bethsaida. To Philip He says, "Follow me," and it is apparent that Philip not only accepted Jesus' call, but he went right out and found a friend, Nathanael, and told him he had found the Messiah and that He was Jesus of Nazareth. Nathanael's derisive response, "Can there any good thing come out of Nazareth?" (1:41) was answered by Philip in the best possible way: "Come and see." The dialogue between Jesus and Nathanael is intriguing (1:47–51). Jesus begins by complimenting him on his integrity and faithfulness to his Hebrew heritage. And from there Jesus led Nathanael along until he recognized the One from Nazareth as "the Son of God...the king of Israel" (1:49).

The interchange between Jesus and Nathanael ties the disclosure of the Christ, the Messiah, to Old Testament prophecies. It is likely that Jesus' comment about seeing Nathanael "under the fig tree" (1:48) is a reference to the Messianic time spoken of so poetically by the prophet Micah (4:3–4) when everyone could study Scripture under his own vine and fig tree. Possibly Nathanael had been doing just that prior to this dramatic meeting. At any rate, he was convinced as to who Jesus was and used two specific Messianic titles in addressing Him—Son of God and King of Israel (1:49).

Jesus is indeed the Son of God—our Lord. This is the declaration of "saving faith" with which all believers are identified. In the days when John wrote this Gospel early Christians were undergoing intense persecution because people within the Roman Empire were commanded to worship the emperor. Each person was asked to declare that Caesar was lord. The Christian response was, "Jesus is Lord, not Caesar." For them, no temporal authority could replace their commitment to Jesus Christ. In similar fashion, we twentieth-century Christians must stand firm in *our* commitment to the Lordship of Christ and not succumb to the temptation in our social and political settings to render to "the Caesars" of our time that which is God's. We are to render to Caesar only what is Caesar's because we must render to God all that is His (Matt. 22:21).

Our Scriptures give us a creation theology. The high points in Scripture regarding creation are Genesis 1–2, John 1, Colossians 1, and Hebrews 1. We learn from these Scriptures that 1) the Creator is distinct from His creation; 2) the Creator made a good world; 3) God created us in the *Imago Dei* (the image of God); 4) sin is an intrusion into the world, a perversion of the good.

The Word—as Creative Act of God.

We learn also that the Christ was promised to come and to correct the perversion of sin and to restore our fellowship with God. Paul wrote that we are predestined "to be conformed to the image" of God's Son (Rom. 8:29). This is not a "creation science" but a creation theology, for science can study the creation but it cannot discover the Creator except through the Creator's own self-disclosure. In reality, the created order, which we know as our universe, is only a "mute witness" of what is interpreted by our Scriptures.

Now, in this part of our Scripture lesson (2:1–11) we are introduced to the creative power of the Son of God. The first verse of John's Gospel identified the Word as "with God, and the Word was God." Next, in verses 2 and 3 we learned that the Word was with God in the beginning, and "all things were made by him..."

John now introduces us to the first of seven of Jesus' miracles—signs—which he gives us in his Gospel: the act of turning water into wine. This is the "sign" of the creative Word personified in Jesus of Nazareth. We see Him here as the Creator Lord, and His act discloses His glory to the disciples, and from this early stage the disciples began to see Jesus as their Messiah (2:11). John's reference to Jesus' glory here reminds us of his earlier witness, "...we beheld his glory, the glory as of the only begotten of the Father (1:14)." This sign shows us the plenteous supply of God's grace. It reminds us of Elijah's miracle in supplying the widow with meal and oil (1 Kings 17:1–16). It is also reminiscent of Elisha's miracles, when he supplied oil for a widow and her sons (2 Kings 4:1–7) and loaves for the people (2 Kings 4:42–44).

Many wedding sermons have been preached from these verses, for Jesus graced the wedding at Cana with His presence. Marriage is to be sanctified by God's presence and purpose. And two people in love should enter marriage in faith and integrity, knowing that the spiritual vitality for their success is the presence of the Christ—in Him they are never alone. And the dynamic of Christian community is in our relating to one another in and through Christ. This means that we do not relate without Him lest we intimidate, manipulate, dominate, or coerce one another. Instead we relate to others in freedom through Him.

There is a tradition that the wedding that day in Cana may have been in the family of Zebedee, and that Zebedee's wife Salome was a sister to Mary, the mother of Jesus. This may explain Mary's special feeling of concern over the wine shortage and why she came to Jesus for help. It isn't likely ahead of time that Mary knew what Jesus would do, but it is obvious that she trusted Him.

Jesus' response to His mother in verse 4 sounds abrupt, but it could have just as well been translated, "Woman, what have you and I to do with that?" (The original word translated "woman" was really a title of respect, although to us, it, too, sounds abrupt.) Jesus then added, "My hour is not yet come" (2:4), and this could mean that it wasn't yet time for Him to act either to show His glory or to not intervene until the situation became actually hopeless.

But we read next that Jesus did act by instructing the servants to fill six large stone jars to the brim with water. He then told them to "Draw out now" from the jars and take the contents—the water that had become wine—to the "ruler of the feast" (2:6–8). The reaction of the "head waiter" in the story is highly significant as he discovers that this wine was so much better than the wine which had been served earlier (2:9–10), for he asked the bridegroom why he had saved the best for the last.

There are several lessons for us in this remarkable story. First, it would have been terribly embarrassing for a Jewish host to have run out of wine before the wedding celebration was over. But Jesus, always sensitive to the feelings and needs of people, stepped in and prevented that embarrassment through His gracious act.

Then, it is significant that Jesus is a part of this festive occasion honoring the marriage of two friends. Not only was His presence there a blessing to the marriage, but apparently here, as in many later occasions, He was enjoying Himself with people. He evidently mixed and mingled well.

But of primary importance, through Jesus' creative act we have a magnificent symbol of the arrival of the "new wine of God's new kingdom"—the new fellowship of believers in Jesus Christ. It was a time of celebration because in Jesus a new quality has come into our lives (Mark 7:1–24) which stands in stark contrast to the cold and formal rule-following pattern in Judaism.

Our Lord is the Creator; He is active in our lives. And we recognize Him as creating His Church in every culture and time, meeting human needs with creative acts which glorify God the Father.

The evidence of His work of creation is all around us. While walking along the sidewalk in Philadelphia one morning, I came upon a series of footprints in the concrete. As I stood looking at them, the thought occurred to me that I couldn't tell whether the person who made those prints was a woman, a youth, or a man with small feet. But I was certain of one thing: somebody had walked there and left those footprints. In a similar way, as we view God's magnificent creation, we know that Someone was at work here. And as we meet Jesus, we now know what the Creator is like. God is like Jesus, active in His love.

In this next scene we find Jesus and His disciples in Jerusalem to celebrate the Passover as John describes the cleansing of the temple court as an expression of His Messianic authority (2:12–17). God's house is to be a center of worship for everyone, but the impiety and crass materialism of the Jewish religious leaders had led to the cluttering

The Word—as The Messiah.

of the Court of the Gentiles with their business traffic so that the gentiles could not come to worship. The prophet Malachi predicted, "The Lord, whom ye seek, shall suddenly come to his temple...But who may abide the day of his coming?...and he shall purify the sons of Levi" (Mal. 3:1–3). We see in this that the judgment of God hangs over the old order, for the new has come!

In the other Gospels the cleansing of the temple is said to have occurred in the closing days of Jesus' life. Either there were several occasions of cleansing the temple, or John selected this account for an early presentation of the authority of Jesus. John in his Gospel chose to emphasize the cleansing of the temple and the zeal for the house of God which motivated Jesus. In Mark's Gospel we have the words, "Is it not written, My house shall be called of all nations the house of prayer?" (Mark 11:17), as an expression of Jesus' concern for all.

This event is used by some to argue that Jesus resorted to violence, thereby justifying the use of violence in human conflict. But this would contradict Jesus' strategy of love in His Sermon on the Mount, for He taught that we should turn the other cheek.

It would appear that Jesus made the whip to drive out the sheep and the oxen. He overturned the tables of the money changers, and verbally denounced those who were guilty of misusing the temple. But there is no proof that He laid the whip on any person. It is true from what John has written that Jesus was angry, but His anger was directed at a system that permitted worshippers to be taken advantage of and the house of God to be desecrated. In other words, I don't believe Jesus' anger was provoked by people. Actually, anger comes from within. The common expression, "He gets my goat" or "She makes me mad" is a fallacy. No one can do that to us without *our* permission. For Jesus, turning the other cheek was His strategy, for He did not allow the behavior of others to determine His response. Instead, He decided His course of action on the basis of His understanding of God's will.

This dramatic event marked the first of three Passover celebrations mentioned by John in this Gospel (the other two are found in 6:4 and 13:1). From this we would understand that Jesus' ministry was approximately three years.

Quite naturally Jesus' action in clearing the temple that day of the merchants and money changers created quite a commotion. And His timing was ideal—the city of Jerusalem and the temple was crowded with pilgrims who were there to observe the Passover. It is quite understandable that His action would be challenged. And afterwards the Jewish leaders asked Jesus for a sign of His authority for doing what He did (2:18). They failed to connect Jesus' actions, as the disciples did, with Psalm 69:9 (2:17) and demanded an explanation. Jesus' response identified the center of worship as Himself, emphasizing the presence of God rather than ritual or ceremonies. John tells us that He spoke of His own body when He said, "Destroy this temple, and in three days I will raise it up" (2:19, 21). Then in verse 22 John further says that following the resurrection of Jesus the disciples understood the Scripture and His words. But the Jewish leaders thought He was referring to Herod's temple which had by then been under construction forty-six years. Instead of understanding His words as a sign of His authority, they thought He was playing games with them.

John tells us that "...many believed in his name, when they saw the miracles which he did" (2:23). This suggests John's awareness of other miracles Jesus performed during the Passover time and later, but he selected seven to illustrate the teaching he was led of the Spirit to share. It is interesting to note that John uses a distinctive Greek word for "miracle" which really means "sign." He saw Jesus' miracles as far more than unusual and isolated actions. Instead, they were signs of what God was really like.

While it was true that "many believed in his name," John now tells us that Jesus was cautious and maintained a reserve because He knew they lacked a full faith commitment. The Greek word for belief in verse 23, *pisteuein*, is also used in verse 24 to say that Jesus "did not commit himself unto them"—He did not trust Himself to them. This helps us understand the same word which is also found in John 3:16, "...that whosoever believeth in him"— whoever *commits* himself to Him, "should not perish but have everlasting life." We are called to a belief that commits, that identifies with Jesus. Dietrich Bonhoeffer, German martyr under Hitler, said that only one who believes truly obeys, and only one who obeys truly believes!

The Christian life is a new beginning, a new relationship with God, a new Master, a new purpose, a new spirit.

The Word—as Regenerating Lord.

Jesus calls it a new birth. Being born from above means to have a new life generated within us through the Spirit of God. In contrast to what we do, in the practice of religion, the new birth is something that happens to us. We are to "be born again," we don't "born ourselves." The new life is the new relation with the Lord; we are reconciled to Him! And this is a corrective for our sinfulness. As a little boy said, "I have something inside of me that I can't do what I want to with."

We come now in our lesson to the fascinating story of Jesus' discussion with Nicodemus (3:1–21). John begins by telling us that Nicodemus instigated the discussion. This was amazing because Nicodemus was a Pharisee, an aristocrat, and a member of the Jewish Sanhedrin—he was one of seventy members of the "Supreme Court." And even though he came to Jesus in the dark of night there was a ring of honesty in his opening comment, "Rabbi, we know that thou art a teacher come from God: for no man can do these miracles that thou doest, except God be with him" (3:2). In spite of his position, he came to talk with Jesus about the kingdom of God.

Jesus opened His part of the conversation by giving Nicodemus a shock treatment, "Except a man be born again, he cannot see the Kingdom of God" (3:3). Jesus is telling Nicodemus and us that knowledge about the Kingdom of God is not enough—he and we must experience a new birth of the Spirit. We are totally dependent on God's grace in being reconciled to Him.

Jesus told Nicodemus twice that he needed to be born from above, born of the Spirit (3:3, 5). The second statement was in response to Nicodemus' question as to how he could start over: "How can a man be born when he is old? Can he enter the second time into his mother's womb?" Jesus replied that each of us has had a "water birth," a physical birth, but He is speaking of a second birth, a spiritual birth. Some commentators see Jesus' reference to being born of water as a reference to baptism, as with John the Baptist, and the spiritual birth as that baptism with the Spirit foretold by the Baptist. But I'm satisfied with the simple contrast between a physical and a spiritual birth in answer to Nicodemus' question in verse 4.

Jesus then went on to describe birth by the Spirit by saying it is like the movement of the wind. Just as we don't see the wind but we see what it does, so we don't see the

Spirit but see rather what He does in a person's life. Zwingli, the great Reformation preacher, described it this way, "There are two baptisms, the outer baptism with water and the inner baptism with the Spirit. The outer baptism doesn't save a person but the inner baptism with the Spirit saves or changes a person."

The words, "The kingdom of God," or the rule of God, appear only here (3:3) and in chapter 18:36 in John's Gospel. However, this term is very prominent in Matthew, Mark, and Luke—especially in Matthew. But John rivets our attention on the Person of the King, under whose rule we are as members of His kingdom, His new fellowship of believers. Paul wrote, "The kingdom of God is not meat and drink; but righteousness, and peace, and joy in the Holy Ghost" (Rom. 14:17).

As the conversation with Nicodemus continues, Jesus is very attentive to his questions, and He moves on to interpret for him the nature of spiritual life and lifts an illustration from His knowledge of the Old Testament. Identifying Himself as the "Son of Man" in the kingdom of heaven (3:13), He foretells His suffering and death (3:14). When Moses lifted up the brazen serpent in the wilderness so that people looking at it in faith wouldn't die (Num. 21:9), they were made aware that the God asking for this symbol of their death experience was their Healer. In this same way, Jesus said, He would be "lifted up" so that people would see beyond Him (the human expression of God's grace) the very act and Person of God!

Now follows what we know as the golden text of the Bible, John 3:16. These few words express the Good News. "God so loved the world"—the breadth of His love—"that he gave his only begotten son"—the length to which His love has gone—"that whosoever believeth in him"—the depth of His love—"should not perish, but have everlasting life"—the height of His love (*see* Eph. 3:18). Central in these words is the reference to Jesus as God's "only begotten Son." The reference here is not only to the Incarnation of God in Jesus but also to God giving up His Son on the Cross (Isa. 53:12). Two important truths emerge in verse 17: we have the identification of Jesus as "Son" in relation to "the Father." Also, the word of grace is that God's purpose is not to judge but to save.

John now moves on to give us an interpretation of salvation (3:18–21). Here the focus is on our believing in the

Christ as the Son of God. John uses the word "believe" ninety-eight times in his Gospel, highlighting the truth that we are saved by a faith relationship with Christ, our reconciliation with God!

Again John's words take us back to an opening statement in his Gospel, "In him was life; and the life was the light of men" (1:4). John combines light with its meaning of truth, for God's truth is the light of life. The contrast between the saved and the lost is the contrast between walking in the light and walking in darkness. We are children of light as we walk in the truth of Christ (3:21).

But there's a paradox here—too much light is no light at all. When we search for an object by flashlight on a dark night, we may succeed. But if we use a flood light we may become so dazzled and blinded that we cannot see. It was for this reason that God came in Jesus, revealing Himself in human form so that we could actually see Him. The dazzling and awesome glory of the eternal God would have been more than humankind could grasp. But here we see what God is like in the Person of Jesus Christ.

The Word—as The Son of God.

The witness of John the Baptist is of special importance in the identification of Jesus as the long-promised Messiah. John burst upon the scene as a flaming prophet. His ministry strongly influenced that whole part of the country. People went in droves to hear him preach and baptize. Regarded by most of the people as a prophet, his words about Jesus were God's sovereign plan for the introduction of Jesus as the Christ, the Messiah. When John was asked whether he himself was the Messiah, his answer was to point to Jesus as the Anointed One, the Messiah.

John said:

> I am not the Christ; I'm sent to announce him! (3:28)
> I am the attendant; he is the bridegroom. (3:29)
> I listen and rejoice; he speaks. (3:29)
> I am enlightened; he is the light of life. (1:6–9)
> I must decrease; he must increase. (3:30)

This part of our lesson (3:22–36) begins with a reference about Jesus' going from Jerusalem into the territory of Judea, probably in the neighborhood of Jordan but to the north of Jerusalem toward Samaria. Jesus and His disciples were now baptizing—apparently the actual performance of the rite was administered by the disciples only

(4:2). The Jewish reporters informed John the Baptist of this, and added, "All men come to him" (3:26). The depth of John's commitment is seen in his response, for having been the one to whom "all Judea and the surrounding regions" had responded, he now saw "his following" turn to Jesus. But he insisted that was the way it should be; people are not to follow the preacher but the Christ (3:30).

John used the illustration of marriage to say that he was only the best man, the friend of the bridegroom—it is the groom that receives the bride. Biblical preaching introduces people not simply to content but to Christ. The skeptic, Hume, said of John Brown of Haddington, "Yon's the man for me, he preaches as if Jesus Christ were at his very elbow."

The final section in this chapter and of our Scripture lesson, verses 31–36, follow as though they are the words of John the Baptist. However, they sound very much like the words of Jesus in the conclusion of His discussion with Nicodemus. This is seen in a comparison of 3:18 with 3:31, 35; "He that cometh from above is above all:...The Father loveth the Son and hath given all things into his hand." This suggests that the words may be those of the Apostle John, the one who is bringing together the Gospel account. This is a remarkable statement contrasting the earthly and the heavenly (3:31); expressing the testimony of knowing the truth of God (3:32–33); emphasizing the unlimited way in which the Spirit filled the life of Jesus (3:34); and presenting the relation of the Father and the Son (3:35). In fact, verse 35 is a parallel passage to the emphasis in Matthew 11:27 of the relationship of Father and Son.

This remarkable section concerning the Deity of Christ emphasized 1) Jesus having come from heaven, 2) His speaking from a first-hand relationship with the Father, 3) His speaking "the words of God," 4) His full identification with the Spirit, and 5) His full endowment with God's power as the extension of Father-Son love (3:31–35). As God's Son, Jesus always did the things that pleased the Father.

Believing in the Son and identifying with Him gives us everlasting life. Fifty billion years from now I expect to be a young man living on with God! This is the quality of life which we have in Christ—it never ends. In contrast, one who does not identify with Christ misses life (3:36b). God's wrath is His respect for our freedom to say "no" to Him without approving our "no." God's wrath and God's

31

love are two sides of the same coin—it is His sovereign control that will not violate our personalities while respecting our freedom for response. Our salvation is by His grace, His taking the initiative and moving to us. But God has moved, He has come to us in Christ; it is our move next.

Rowland Hill, the great British preacher, as an old man of 84 was heard singing to himself, as he walked up and down the aisles of Surrey Chapel, these words,

> When I am to die, receive me I'll cry
> For Jesus has loved me, I cannot tell why;
> But this I do find, we two are so joined,
> He'll not be in heaven and leave me behind.

This is the Jesus John introduces us to in this first lesson.

Father, Thank You for loving the world so much that You gave Your only begotten Son that we might have eternal life. AMEN.

WHAT THIS SCRIPTURE MEANS TO ME—John 1–3

"The Eagle Gospel, the one that soars above." I have written those words opposite the first page of the Gospel of John in my Bible. John, looking back from the vantage point of many years, wrote, under the inspiration of the Holy Spirit, the Gospel that makes the others complete.

These three opening chapters are rich in truth. But three words trumpet their special message for me: *Light, Life, and Love.*

In the opening verses of the Gospel John tells us that Jesus is "the light of men," and then the writer adds a profound truth in verse 5—the brilliant light of Jesus has never been extinguished. Instead, where the light of Jesus shines, the very darkness becomes light. Those are comforting words when darkness seems to be overpowering the world and people everywhere appear to have lost their bearings.

Boris Kornfeld was a Russian Jew, a medical doctor and a Christian. In the vast obscenity of the Gulag where he was a political prisoner, he came to know Jesus as his Saviour.

One night Dr. Kornfeld shared the good news of the gospel with a fellow prisoner, a man with advanced cancer. Later that same night the doctor was murdered by a cruel guard who he had reported for stealing bread intended for the desperately ill pellagra patients. The tiny little light that had shown in the vast darkness of the prison camp had been extinguished, or so the guard thought. But the cancer patient lived and he, too, became a Christian. His name is Aleksandr Solzhenitsyn, considered by many to be the foremost writer of this century.

Life is the second word that has special meaning for me, and right at the beginning (1:4) John tells us that "In him was life." And later Jesus Himself underscored that truth when He said, "I am come that they might have life..." (10:10). Then, it isn't long before we are introduced to a man whose life was so transformed when he met Jesus, that while he stumbled at times, he was never the same again. When Jesus met Simon, He looked deeply into his soul and gave him a new name, "...thou shalt be called Cephas"—Peter. As you know, these names mean "rock."

I've often wondered what Simon's friends thought about his new name. They had to know from his actions that he wasn't very rock-like. Even after being with Jesus for over three years Peter was still soft and unpredictable in moments of crisis. In the garden when Jesus was arrested it was Peter who drew his sword and sliced off the ear of one of the temple guards. And later in the courtyard of the high priest after Jesus' arrest, it was Peter who insisted that he didn't even know who Jesus was. At this time of Peter's life he was more like crumbly Texas shale than rock-like. But, happily, Jesus didn't see Peter as the man he was, but as the man he would become.

Peter, though, is still my favorite disciple; he is so human, and I'm so much like him. I, too, have the tendency to act on the spur of the moment and to get my foot in my mouth. In my zeal I may, without thinking, dash off to church every time the door is open when in reality I probably should be at home now and then to bake some of the goodies my husband loves so much.

But I have faith to believe that when Jesus looks into the depths of my own soul, He will see something of what He saw in Peter—one who loves Him and is in the process of becoming, with His help, what He intends for me to be. This is the assurance of our faith—Christ *alive* in us even in the turbulent days in which we live.

And now we come to that third word which is so much a part of this lesson—*Love*. "For God so LOVED the world..." John 3:16 is perhaps the best-known and best-loved verse in the entire New Testament. While traveling down a Texas highway several years ago, the real meaning of that verse came to me in a new way. Somehow, while driving alone in the car, I was overwhelmed with the thought that if I had been the only person to have ever lived, Jesus Christ, God's only Son, would have died just for me.

This awesome thought swept back and forth through my body like an ocean wave. While we don't deserve it, and we can't earn it, God loves us!

LESSON 2
JOHN 4–6

Christ, the Reconciler— by Faith

Dear God, As I read this lesson, awaken within me the measure of faith You've already given me. AMEN.

Someone has defined faith as "Forsaking All I Trust Him!" Faith is our response to evidence; it is the action of our will when intellect and emotions are motivated by truth.

Actually, saving faith is no different intellectually and psychologically from any other expression of faith. For example, we exercise faith in our friendships, in our marriages—even in our business or professional lives. What makes *saving faith* different is that it is faith in the Saviour.

In our first lesson in the Gospel of John we saw that salvation comes through believing in—having faith in—Jesus Christ. Now, in this lesson John shows us the nature of faith. Here we come to see that faith as response to evidence grows *with* the evidence. It may begin small, but it will grow. In the middle nineteenth century, the State of New York wanted to put a bridge across the Niagara River; $10,000 was offered to the first person who would fly a kite across the gorge. In 1848 Homan Walsh flew a kite across the Niagara River. By using the first light string that was attached to the kite, a slightly heavier string was pulled across. This step was repeated again and again, each time with a larger cord, until finally a strong cable was pulled across. This formed the basic support for the first foot bridge, which had its start with the kite string.

We are indebted to John for this marvelous, yet shocking story of Jesus and the Samaritan woman at Sychar (4:1–26). It is a classic example of the awakening of faith.

The lesson opens with the news that controversy was brewing in Judea because of the success of Jesus' ministry (4:1–2). Rather than confront at that time the growing rancor of the Pharisees, Jesus "left Judea and departed again unto Galilee." But instead of taking the usual route—east to Jericho and across the Jordan River before turning north—Jesus headed directly through the hostile territory of Samaria.

Deep feelings of hatred and bitterness had separated the Jews and the Samaritans for over seven hundred years. When the Northern Kingdom of Israel was invaded and conquered in 722 B.C., the Samaritans had integrated and intermarried with their foreign conquerers and from the Jewish perspective were unclean. For this reason Jewish travelers going north to Galilee nearly always took the eastern route up the Jordan gorge even though it took twice as long. But this time John tells us that Jesus "must needs go through Samaria" (4:4)—a statement of Jesus' sense of mission.

Next, we see Jesus arriving at a fork in the road near the Samaritan city of Sychar. It was noon and hot and Jesus was tired and thristy. While John emphasizes the diety of Jesus throughout his Gospel, he now pictures a very human Jesus, resting by a well while His disciples went into town to obtain food.

It was then that the woman of Sychar came out to Jacob's well to draw water. It may be that she came at noon to avoid the other women who had probably gotten their water earlier in the morning, for as we soon discover, she was a woman of immoral relationships.

Now we witness a marvelous lesson in personal evangelism as Jesus spoke to her and asked a favor, "Give me to drink" (4:7). For Jesus, a Jewish rabbi, to even speak to her defied rabbinical law, and no good Jew would even touch a water vessel belonging to a Samaritan. Her amazement was real, but Jesus responded by talking to her about "living water." And this not only caught her deepest interest, it opened the way for a discussion about the inner life. He was ever sensitive to the needs of people He met, and He

Faith—Its Awakening.

knew her need was great when He asked her to "Go, call thy husband, and come hither" (4:16).

She met this test of honesty when she said, "I have no husband." It was then that Jesus exposed her sin, for she'd had five and the man she was living with then wasn't her husband.

Upon realizing that Jesus was a prophet (4:19), she shifted the conversation to a theological issue. The Samaritans had long insisted that God was to be worshipped on their Mount Gerizim instead of in Jerusalem—which was right? Jesus' response, that "salvation is of the Jews" (4:22), focused on the arrival of the Messiah, and He then moved to declare that the New Order—God's new fellowship—had arrived! The woman apparently followed His train of thought clearly for she immediately referred to her faith in the fact that the Messiah would come and "would tell us all things" (4:25).

It is significant that Jesus' first declaration of Himself as the Messiah was to this Samaritan woman (4:26). She had been honest with Him, and whenever we come in honest faith to God, that faith is confirmed in His gracious acceptance. Her life was transformed, for she left her burden of sin for a new moral start. She left her religion based on a *place*, for faith in a *Person*, and she left her bitter spirit for a new freedom and joy.

When Jesus told her and us that "God is a Spirit: and they that worship him must worship him in spirit and in truth" (4:24), He made it clear that God is Spirit-being in contrast to physical-being. Our worship is a reality of our spirits and not primarily of religious rites. Our worship "in Spirit and in truth" is elaborated in Matthew's account of the Sermon on the Mount where Jesus moves us beyond act to attitude, beyond form to fellowship. And faith moves us to fellowship with God and our "neighbors" nearby and across the world.

Faith—Its Response.

The gospel song, "Fill My Cup, Lord," is an expression of the response of faith built on the story of the Samaritan woman at the well. Many persons look for an answer to their hunger for God through pursuing selfish goals. But our hunger for God will never be satisfied with anything but Him. Anselm of Canterbury prayed:

Help us to seek Thee in longing,
And long for Thee in seeking;
To find Thee in loving,
And love Thee in finding.

In these next verses (4:27–42) we see three expressions of the response of faith: 1) in the Samaritan woman; 2) in the disciples of Jesus; and 3) in the Samaritan people. In each case the disclosure of Jesus' Messianic role brought out a faith response.

The woman went back into the city of Sychar a changed person. She left her empty waterpot for a new life of inner fullness as she told the men of the city, "Come, see a man, which told me all things that ever I did: is not this the Christ?" (4:29). She left her burden of guilt for a new freedom of grace. And she left her poor self-image for a positive witness of faith. Now, as then, we cannot *really* be with Jesus and remain the same, and we cannot *really* be with Jesus without sharing, as this woman did, the Good News of new life in Him.

It certainly isn't surprising that when the disciples returned from the city, they were amazed to find Jesus sitting by the well in a public place and talking to the Samaritan woman (4:27). This just wasn't done! The rabbis taught that a man never talked to a woman on the street—not even his own wife. Once again, Jesus defied custom to meet human need—people, not rules, were important to Him.

Next, the disciples urged Jesus to eat the food they had brought back with them, but He declined saying, "I have meat to eat that ye know not of" (4:32). Once again, they failed to understand and wondered among themselves whether someone had brought Him something to eat while they were away (4:33). This, of course, wasn't the case. What He was trying to help them see was that His food—His source of strength—came from doing the will and work of His Father. Two other times in John's Gospel Jesus refers to the work His Father gave Him to do—5:36 and 17:4.

Now Jesus gave the disciples an insight into the mission of the Kingdom of God and what their response to faith should be (4:35–38). Drawing on an analogy of sowing and reaping, Jesus points out that beginning with John the Baptist the seed of the gospel was being sown—now was a time of reaping, "Lift up your eyes, and look on the fields; for they are white already to harvest" (4:35). They were being called into God's harvest field.

There is an important message for us today in these words of Jesus. There are 4.7 billion people in our world, and it is estimated that 2.7 billion have not yet heard the Good News of the gospel of Jesus Christ. Then add to that members of our families, people in our neighborhoods and in our towns and cities, who do not know Jesus as Saviour and Lord—indeed our fields today are white and ready for the harvest. To meet this challenge it is important that we hear Jesus' emphasis on the team approach—as we work together, one sows and another reaps. By working this way our witness is complete and we avoid the individualism that measures success by our own achievements. In reality, our response of faith is to be faithful and leave the measure of success up to God.

In verses 39–42 we have the response of the Samaritan people to Jesus. First, John tells us that "many of the Samaritans of that city believed on him" because of the woman's testimony (4:39). Then the believing Samaritans went to see Jesus for themselves and were so impressed that they asked Him to stay with them for a time—and He did, for two days (4:40). And during those two days they came to really believe because of Jesus' own words (4:41–42). As it was with them—so it is with us. We cannot exist on a borrowed faith—a true response of faith comes through personal commitment.

A friend of mine told me about attending church as a boy, of going to a Christian college, and then completing his education by earning a doctorate. But through all of that he had never experienced a personal relationship with Jesus Christ. After leaving the university, he began practicing his vocation in a small town in West Virginia where he taught Sunday school in a little Methodist church. During a series of special meetings he went forward to the altar and committed his life to Christ. When he arose from his knees and looked around, he saw that his entire Sunday school class of boys was at the altar with him. What a thrill that was as he passed from a secondhand religion to a firsthand spiritual experience!

John closes this marvelous story with the acknowledgment of the new Samaritan Christians that Jesus was indeed the Christ—the Messiah—the Saviour of the world.

What a grand climax to Jesus' days in the village of Sychar! He had stopped as He traveled for a rest, for a drink, and for a noon meal at Jacob's well. But there He met deep human need and interrupted His travel north to meet that need. People in need were never an interruption to Jesus—and they should not be an interruption to us. Our busyness must never get in the way of God's business.

Faith is response to evidence, and these next verses (4:43–54) focus on the integrity of the response. When we believe in the Person and victory of Christ, we glorify Him by acknowledging His actions and by acclaiming His authority.

Faith—Its Integrity.

When we pray in Jesus' name we don't try to order God around as though He were our cosmic bellhop. Rather, through our prayers, we recognize His victory over sin and death by identifying with Him in that victory.

The scene shifts now from Samaria to Galilee where John tells us that Jesus is enthusiastically received (4:45). In Cana, Jesus was confronted by a nobleman whose son was very ill. This concerned father had traveled the twenty or so miles from his home in Capernaum to find Jesus and ask for His help, "Sir, come down ere my child die" (4:49). Jesus' response was immediate, "Go thy way; thy son liveth."

The nobleman believed Jesus and started the long trek back home. What a vivid contrast between the faith of this man, who was probably a gentile, and the institutional Jewish religious leaders who were always challenging Jesus' acts and authority. The nobleman's simple obedience is a marvelous illustration of the integrity of faith. There is a lesson in this for us that is most important. We must not let the institutionalization of our religious experience keep us from being open to the creative acts of God in our lives.

Jesus' approach to the official's request was first to test the genuineness of his faith, "Except ye see signs and wonders, ye will not believe" (4:48). This is very similar to Jesus' dialogue with the Syrophoenician woman (Mark 7:27). But the father's response revealed the intensity of his pain and anxiety for his dying son and his full dependence upon Jesus. Seeing the father's reaction, Jesus responded with the good news that his son would live. When the nobleman heard this, he didn't demand proof of his son's healing nor did he beg Jesus to lay His hands on his son.

He simply believed and obeyed. This is the true character of faith, the ability to act on the promise!

On his return to Capernaum the official was met by his servants. This appears to have been the day following his request of Jesus, for the servants inform him that at the seventh hour (1:00 P.M.) on the preceding day the fever had left his son. The father realized that the time the boy was cured coincided with the time at which Jesus had announced his healing. What a glad moment this was for the father and his entire family as they saw the evidence of faith in the well boy. The man's faith enabled him to respond to Jesus based on his understanding of Him as the life-giver. Here were living witnesses of John's earlier word, "In him was life; and the life was the light of men" (1:4).

John concludes this story by telling his readers and us that this was the second miracle-sign that "Jesus did, when he was come out of Judea into Galilee" (4:54). It is apparent from this statement that John did not intend to include in his select list of signs the miracles that Jesus performed in Judea (2:23). In the miracles that John did choose, we see illustrations of Christ's acts as creating and sustaining life.

Faith opens new dimensions of life beyond ourselves. As we have faith in one another, our personal lives are expanded. A lack of faith in others confines our lives to ourselves—to engage only in the limited circle of things which we can control.

In like fashion, faith in God opens our lives to all that God offers. The famous philosopher, C.E.M. Joad joined Bertrand Russell, H. G. Wells, and George B. Shaw in an attempt to discredit Christianity. But when he was in his 70's, Joad came to faith in Christ before the inescapable evidence and said, "The one whom I denied all my life I must now embrace!"

Faith is not a crutch, not simply a support for the weakling. Rather, faith is the honest, humble awareness that there is more to life than what we can control and master; it is the privilege of relating our lives to the Reality of Jesus

OPPOSITE. The Pool of Bethesda where the lame man waited for the "troubling of the waters." Excavations have revealed at a very deep level the remains of a portion of two pools from New Testament times. The high arches above it are supports for a later church built over these pools.

Christ that enriches us and gives life its true meaning.

Faith—Its Effect.

We come now to the third sign (miracle) in John's Gospel as he tells us the story about a man who had been an invalid for thirty-eight years (5:1–18). There was a possibility that after being incapacitated for so long he had become accustomed to it. It is a very human tendency to accept ourselves as we are because in so doing we avoid the pain involved in change. Most of us can come up with a dozen and one excuses that justify our condition or position.

We meet this man and Jesus at the Pool of Bethesda in Jerusalem. Evidently, when Jesus saw him He took a deep interest in him. There were doubtless many other disabled people clustered around the pool that day, but this long-term invalid became the object of Jesus' attention.

We next read that Jesus asked the man a rather curious question, "Wilt thou be made whole?" In response the man replied that there wasn't anyone to help him into the healing water. From this, Jesus knew that he was willing for change, and He extended His healing grace with the word of authority, "Rise, take up thy bed and walk" (5:8). At once the man was cured. One word from the Master meets our need, for He is the Word (Logos) of God, and God's creative power is in this Word.

Earlier in our Scripture lesson we learned that there was intermittent moving of the water in the Pool of Bethesda. Some early biblical manuscripts include a sentence stating that people believed that an angel troubled the water and gave it healing powers (5:4), others omit this reference. But the important message for us in this event is that Jesus didn't focus on the water but on the man's need. And in addressing that need the man was healed. Jesus' own faith in the power and work of God was of primary importance. The paralytic's faith to respond to Jesus' word effected a total change. He picked up his bed and strode away (5:9), even though it was the Sabbath and the laws of Sabbath behavior strictly forbad this.

The carping Jewish leaders immediately condemned him for carrying his bed, which they interpreted as working on the Sabbath (5:10). He responded to their attack by telling them that the One who had healed him told him to "Take up thy bed and walk." And when they asked who had healed him, he didn't know (5:12–13). Jesus had left the man whole and had slipped away into the crowd seeking no special attention. What a lesson in contrasts. Jesus had concentrated on the man's need for wholeness while the self-righteous religious leaders concentrated on his violation of the Law.

Later when Jesus met the healed man again He told him to stop sinning lest he experience a worse thing (5:14). No doubt the relation of sin and brokenness is an intended implication of Jesus' statement, but in the largest sense Jesus called the man to a sense of responsibility.

Our difficulties are opportunities for us to experience the power of God. It is for us to decide what it is that we really want God to do for us. When Jesus asks if we want to be made whole, He confronts us with responsible decision. It is for us to refuse the compromise which surrenders to the status quo. The wholeness of God comes to those who seek Him. We will do well to pray with St. Augustine, "Enlarge Thou the mansion of my soul that Thou mayest enter in."

This part of the story closes as the healed man identifies his healer as Jesus and the Jewish religious leaders turn their anger on Him for healing on the Sabbath. And as John writes, they "sought to slay him" (5:16). In response to their vicious attack Jesus makes this striking statement, "My Father worketh hitherto, and I work" (5:17). What a bold statement of faith! The Creator God continues to be at work in the world—creating and sustaining (Heb. 1:3). This is our security—our confidence as we, too, are active in the work of God in our world today.

Faith—Its Assurance.

The Good News of the gospel of Jesus is that we can become children of God. This is what it means to be saved —to be reconciled to God and to be in His family. And this assurance rests on the truth of Jesus. He is as good as His word! Again, we recall these words from the beginning of John's Gospel, "As many as received him, to them gave he the power to become the sons of God" (1:12).

We turn now in our lesson to Jesus' response to the Jewish religious leaders concerning His oneness with God the Father (5:19–47). How do we know that Jesus reconciles us to God? The answer is in His relation with the Father. Jesus ordered His total life and ministry in the will of the Father. Here we see that—

- The Father is the model for the Son (5:19).
- The Father loves the Son and works through Him (5:20).
- The Father gives life to the dead, so the Son gives life (5:21).
- The Father ties His honor to the Son (5:23).

The key verse on assurance in this passage is verse 24, "Verily, verily, I say unto you, He that heareth my word, and believeth on him that sent me, *hath* everlasting life and shall not come into condemnation; but is passed from death unto life" (italics mine). In hearing Jesus and believing on the Father we are given eternal life! Passing "from death to life" is a reference to the nature of salvation, for separated from God we have been spiritually dead (Eph. 2:1a), but in Christ we are made alive (Eph. 2:1b).

And this new life in Christ is both qualitative and quantitative. "For as the Father hath life in himself; so hath he given to the son to have life in himself" (5:26). This verse reminds us again of John's earlier word, "In him was life; and the life was the light of men" (1:4).

Jesus next moves on to give assurance that this life extends into the resurrection (5:29)—that our lives are not bordered by either the cradle or the grave. This says to me that fifty billion years from now I will be a young man living on with God! And this is a fact because of God's grace. It is also made clear in this verse that this resurrection unto *life* is for all who commit themselves to Jesus Christ as Saviour and Lord. It is only those who refuse to believe, like the scribes and Pharisees of Jesus' time, who are condemned. Dr. E. Stanley Jones, missionary to India a generation ago, said one time, "If we will not take from the hand of grace, we will have to take from the hand of judgment."

We also see in these verses that the Father shows the Son everything He does (5:19), everything He thinks (5:22), and everything He wills (5:30–32). And the good news for us is that our relationship to the Son places us in direct relationship with the Father—He is *our* Father. This is an awesome, yet very reassuring word for us.

Jesus then reminds His listeners that John the Baptist witnessed to the truth that He is the Christ but then adds that the authority which the Father has given Him is the greater and final witness (5:36–38). And as further proof of His authority, He states that the "works that I do, bear witness of me, that the Father hath sent me" (5:36). The "works" Jesus is speaking of here are the seven signs (miracles) which John selected to include in his Gospel. These are presented in chapters 2, 4, 5, 6a, 6b, 9, and 11—all are witnesses to His diety.

In the closing verses in this particular section (5:39–47) Jesus' listeners and we are reminded that it is possible to "search the scriptures"—to know the Scriptures—and still miss the Person of whom the Word of God bears witness. His listeners then—the Jewish religious leaders—prided themselves in the knowledge of their Scriptures, yet the love of God was not in them and they were rejecting Him. Instead, they were more concerned about one another's approval than about God's approval. Some years later the Apostle Paul spoke to this when he wrote, "Study to show thyself *approved unto God...*" (2 Tim. 2:15, italics mine).

Finally, we understand from these verses that Jesus holds us accountable for what we know. In the case of Jesus' listeners who professed to know Moses' writings, they would be held accountable for everything that Moses taught, including recognition of the coming of the superior Prophet, the Messiah—Christ. In our case, it isn't religion that matters—Jesus must be taken into account, for only in Him can we actually be reconciled to the Father.

The words of assurance that Jesus has given us here are adequate for every problem and circumstance of life—all we need to do is take Him at His word. Solzhenitsyn in his novel, *One Day in the Life of Ivan Denisovich*, tells about a fellow prisoner, Alyoshka, who was serving a ten-year prison sentence. It soon became apparent that he was different from all the rest of the prisoners—he was a Christian and read his Gospels daily...facing the light bulb!

Faith—Its Provision.

Jesus is the Bread of Life (6:35). In Him and of Him we have our sustenance—everything we need for life. As God supplied manna in the wilderness after the Exodus to sustain the lives of the Israelites, so Jesus is our Bread from heaven, and only as we partake of Him, can we truly *live* (6:1–40).

John now gives the fourth and fifth signs or miracles that are included in his Gospel—the feeding of the 5,000, and Jesus walking on the water (6:1–21). And they are not unre-

The Sea of Galilee. Boats of private fishermen still glean their harvest from the waters of the sea, following in the occupational footsteps of Jesus' disciples.

lated, for the feeding of the 5,000 is a sign that Jesus sustains life, and His walk on the Sea of Galilee is a sign that He secures life.

When God appeared to Moses in the desert in the burning bush, He gave His name as Yahweh, the One "I Am," self-determined Presence. In this Gospel John presents Jesus as using the same expression: "I am the bread of life"; "I am the light of the world"; "I am the good shepherd"; "I am the door"; "I am the resurrection and the life"; "I am the vine"; "I am the Son of God"; "I am the way, the truth, and the life." There are additional expressions that can be added to this list, such as Jesus' response to the Samaritan woman's comment about the Messiah, "I that speak unto thee am he," and His answer to Pilate's question as to whether He was a king, "Thou sayest that I am a king." From all of this, we see that Jesus was clear about His mission, and we, too, need to be clear about our involvement in the Father's will.

These two signs occurred in the region of Galilee (6:1). First, John tells us about the crowds that thronged Jesus because of "his miracles which he did on them that were diseased" (6:2), and then we see Him as He takes the twelve

The Sea of Galilee. Here around the northern shore are set many of the stories of Jesus' ministry. Tradition has it that it wasn't far from here where Jesus fed the 5,000.

disciples up in a mountain for a time of teaching. But it wasn't long before the crowd found them. They had probably walked several miles in their effort to catch up with Jesus, and when He saw them coming, His heart went out to them with compassion—also He had a plan (6:6). John sets this sign in relationship with the Passover (6:4), identifying what He knew was about to happen in the providing of food with the mercy of God in Israel's deliverance.

After Jesus had tested Philip (6:5–7), Andrew entered the scene with a boy and his lunch of five barley loaves and two small fish (6:8–9). Now Jesus acted in faith as He gave instructions for the crowd to be seated. He then took the boy's meager lunch, gave thanks for it, and it was distributed to the entire crowd. John then tells us that when everyone had eaten their fill, the disciples gathered up twelve baskets of fragments. In this scene Jesus modeled by His faith in the Father how we are to believe in Him. Our little, given in faith to God, can become much as He multiplies it for His purposes.

John now moves us right on to the fourth sign (6:14–21). The well-fed crowd had been so impressed by Jesus' miracle-sign that they wanted to crown Him king, but Jesus slipped away quietly alone into an isolated place. When evening came, the disciples decided to return the few miles by ship to Capernaum without Jesus. As they were crossing, a strong wind swept across the Sea of Galilee, and while they were struggling against it, they saw "Jesus walking on the sea" toward them. John tells us, "...they were afraid" until Jesus said, "It is I; be not afraid" (6:20).

In these two events—the feeding of the 5,000 and the meeting of Jesus with His disciples on the sea—we see signs of God's gracious acts in the sharing of His life and Himself with us now, even as He did with the crowds and the disciples then. And God's acts are never capricious but are always tied to the way He has worked throughout all history.

The next day while talking with the crowds that had gathered again, Jesus builds on these two miracle-signs by reminding the people of Moses. He explained, though, that it was not Moses, but God through Moses who had provided their bread in the wilderness and who now sent the true Bread of Life (6:35), and if we believe in Him, we will never hunger or thirst again!

Augustine immortalized this whole thought when he

A view of ruins in Capernaum. It was in the synagogue here that Jesus delivered the discourse found in John 6:22-66.

wrote, "For Thy glory we were and are created, and our hearts are restless until they find their rest in Thee." In each of us there is a hunger for God that can never be satisfied with mere things.

The provision of grace is expressed in the familiar words of verse 37, "All that the Father giveth me shall come to me: and him that cometh to me I will in no wise cast out"—that promise is for each of us, here and now. In faith we can come to Him with the certainty that He receives us, and it is in this faith that we can rest confidently.

The writer of the book of Hebrews put it this way, "There remaineth therefore a rest to the people of God. For he that is entered into his rest, he also hath ceased from his own works, as God did from his" (Heb. 4:9–10). God stopped His work at the time of Creation, not because He was tired but because He was finished. We now can stop our striving and struggle and rest in the finished work of Christ. Dr. Thomas Dooley, missionary to Laos, said shortly before his death at the age of thirty-five, "I believe the important thing is not how long we live, but what we do with the days allotted to us."

Faith—Its Discernment. There is a unique voluntarism about the Christian faith. Salvation is by grace—by God's initiative and provision. And our faith is a voluntary response to God's action. But God always takes the initiative. He moved first by coming to us in Christ. Now, as we face the truth of God in Jesus, we either respond in belief to identify with Him or in a disbelief that rejects Him.

In this closing part of our lesson (6:41–71) Jesus builds on all He has said and done up to this point, first by responding publicly (6:59) to the murmuring and questioning of the Jews and then in private to the twelve disciples. It was clear then as it is now that not everyone is open to God's truth. When Jesus further interpreted the meaning of His redemptive mission as the "Bread of Life," many turned away (6:66). When that happened Jesus then turned to the twelve disciples and asked, "Will ye also go away?" (6:67).

To that piercing question, Simon Peter answered in words reminiscent of his great confession at Caesarea Philippi (Matt. 16:16), "Lord, to whom shall we go? thou hast the words of eternal life. And we believe and are sure that thou art the Christ, the Son of the living God" (6:68–69). In these words we have the conclusion to which each of us is led in the discernment of faith: when we want to know God, we find Him in Jesus.

We see a vivid contrast in this part of our Scripture lesson between the Jewish minds who could not hear Jesus because of their prejudice, and the disciples who heard Him. And Jesus identifies and highlights this problem of prejudice—of lacking discernment of faith—by pointing out that even one of His own disciples was an antagonist and betrayer (6:70–71).

The character of their unbelief is shown in their arguments with the claims of Jesus. The prejudiced always have arguments for their position. The arguments of the Jewish religious leaders were 1) How can He claim to have come from heaven? We know His parents (6:42); 2) How can He give us His flesh to eat (6:52); 3) This is a difficult teaching, who can accept this? (6:60). Disbelief can be changed to belief only by openness to the evidence, and they refused to be open.

Jesus then presented the basis for a discerning faith in His answers to the Jews. First He built on the truth expressed in the early verses of the Gospel, "... the law was given by Moses, but grace and truth came by Jesus Christ" (1:17) by saying, 1) Salvation by grace is seen in the primacy of God's call (6:44); 2) No one can claim to know God and ignore His Son (6:44); 3) No one has seen the Father, but the Son, so a full knowledge of God comes only in Christ (6:46); 4) Christ is the living Bread from heaven, the source of eternal life (6:50); 5) The life Jesus spoke of was the life of spirit in contrast to the flesh—a life of fellowship with God (6:63–64).

Also found in this particular Scripture lesson are two important theological truths. First, God's sovereign grace is expressed in 6:44 and 6:65. Second, the meaning of the Incarnation is expressed in 6:46, 51, 57, and 62. You may want to re-read these Scriptures now in your *Working Bible*.

We began our lesson by defining faith: Forsaking *All I Trust Him*. We close the lesson with this summary. Faith is deciding where to invest our lives. Faith discerns truth and acts upon it. Faith involves the total person—the mind in discernment, the emotions in devotion, and the will in decision. And like Peter, we are led to affirm, "Lord...you have the words of eternal life...."

Lord God, You gave new life to the woman at the well, the nobleman's son, the crippled man at Bethesda—thank You for giving new life to me! AMEN.

WHAT THIS SCRIPTURE MEANS TO ME—John 4–6

"To walk with Jesus through these three chapters of our Scripture lesson leaves me breathless. First we see Him moving north from Judea into Samaria where He meets the woman at the well. From there He goes to Galilee where He heals the Jewish official's son. Then we follow Him back to Jerusalem where He heals the man at the pool of Bethesda. Next, we find Him in the temple teaching the great truth about who He is. Finally, the scene shifts back to the Galilean hills where He feeds the multitude and teaches the vast throng that follows Him. In every place we find Jesus meeting human needs—physical and spiritual—touching bodies and healing hearts.

But I am particularly drawn to the words, "And he must needs go through Samaria," and the encounter that follows. This scene and Jesus' words speak to me in a special way because of an experience in my own life.

Not long ago a call came to me from a woman in Montgomery, Alabama. She had sat next to a physician friend of ours at a dinner party, and as people so often do, she had asked him for medical advice about her daughter who was temporarily living in our city. The doctor told her that he had friends there, and gave her my name.

In desperation she called and asked if I would please check on her daughter who had been sick, was jobless, and had no car, telephone, or friends. In response to this woman's cry for help I told her I would go see her daughter.

When I drove to the address that had been given me, I discovered it was on a sleazy, run-down street where neglected apartments are sandwiched in between topless bars. Like the Jews of Jesus' day, I would gladly have gone miles out of my way to avoid being seen after sunup on Third Street.

As I stopped in front of a nondescript house that was badly in need of paint, two thoughts raced through my mind: what in the world am I doing here? and, I hope she isn't home—then I can just leave a note. But she was home, and I was trapped.

We sat on her porch and talked. I gave her a jar of homemade applesauce; she thanked me and said she hadn't eaten all day.

The next day I took her grocery shopping.

Yesterday I took her to the Family Clinic for a physical checkup. Her bravado broke down on the way home. As tears poured down her cheeks, she told me how scared she was. I held her in my arms for a long time.

It would be easy to condemn her. Her straw-colored hair showed an inch of darkened roots, her heavy makeup was ineptly applied, and her boisterous, flirty

52

manner bugled a lifestyle that I don't approve of. But slowly I began to see that condemning her and writing her off would be tantamount to the behavior of the judgmental legalists of Jesus' day, whom He repeatedly chastised. To follow in His way means to practice His presence. And practicing His presence means showing the gentle, healing love that Jesus showed the Samaritan woman as He pointed her to the "living water."

Tomorrow I'm taking Jo some stationery, but not the kind she asked me for. "Just any old stuff," she'd said. "I don't even care if the envelopes match, but I need to write my mom. I know she is worried about me." Somehow Jo needs to know that she is worth a lot more than a pretty box of stationery with matching envelopes, but that is a start.

Perhaps, too, tomorrow will be the day that we will get beyond her surface problems and she will find the living water that Jesus so lovingly offered to the woman at the well...and that He still offers to my newfound friend on Third Street.

LESSON 3
JOHN 7–9

Christ, the Reconciler— in Freedom

Dear God, Open my heart and mind to the truths in this lesson. AMEN.

Receiving Jesus as Saviour means freedom: "If the Son therefore shall make you free, ye shall be free indeed" (8:36).

There is the freedom to be God's child; the freedom in the fellowship of the Spirit. Consequently, there is freedom *from* self-centeredness, freedom *from* sin, *to* worship. The quality of this freedom, though, results not in lawlessness but in personal choice. For example, if the doctor placed a handful of vitamin capsules on the table and said, "You are free to take all that you choose to take, but you should know that there are several that contain poison," you are not really free. On the other hand, if he says, "Help yourself, only avoid the red ones because there is poison in those," then you really have the freedom to choose properly. That's the way it is with law and grace—God's grace frees us to choose while at the same time it holds us responsible.

Freedom—in Recognizing Truth. This part of our lesson (7:1–36) opens with John telling us that opposition to Jesus by the Jewish religious leaders had become so violent that He was now under the threat of death (7:1). For this reason He stayed close by the region of Galilee where their influence was not so strong.

But we next read in verse 2 that the eight-day Festival of

Tabernacles was at hand. This occurred around the middle of October, and every good Jew, if he could manage it at all, wanted to celebrate this festival in Jerusalem. Knowing this, Jesus' brothers, who at that time didn't really believe in Him, rather cynically urged Him to go to Jerusalem and give a public demonstration of His power. Up to that time all His miracle-signs had occurred in Galilee.

It is significant to note at this point that while John's Gospel does not give us Jesus' temptation experiences in the wilderness, all three temptations are shown as present in His life. You recall that in the wilderness temptation event Satan offered Jesus all the kingdoms of the world (Matt. 4:8; Luke 4:5–7), and in John 6:15 the people wanted to make Him king. Next, Satan invited Jesus to satisfy His hunger by turning the stones into bread (Matt. 4:3; Luke 4:3), and in John 6:30–31 the people asked for miraculous bread. And, finally, Satan in the wilderness experience took Jesus to the temple pinnacle and suggested that He jump off to show His power (Matt. 4:5–6; Luke 4:9–11), and here in John 7:3 His brothers urge Him to go to Jerusalem and demonstrate His power for all to see.

In response to His brothers' urging Jesus said, "My time is not yet come" (7:6). The word for "time" that Jesus used here is unique to this conversation—it actually means the proper time or "opportunity." He is telling them that for Him to leave at that moment would not be timely—for His purposes. Instead, as we shall see, it would be better for Him to go a little later so He could move into the scene quietly and select His own timing for action. Jesus stood free among His brothers and associates then and always to make decisions on the basis of His perception of the will of God.

John now gives us, almost parenthetically, the reactions of the crowd in Jerusalem as they looked for Him (7:11–13). Some said that He was a good man, but then, inconsistently, they failed to take His teachings seriously. Others argued that He was a deceiver and refused to hear His claims of being the Son of God. But whatever the perception, we read that fear of others prevented them from openly affirming that He was the Christ. The important lesson for us in this is that when confronted by Jesus we cannot be neutral—we are either for Him or against Him.

John's reference to the hostility of the Jews in seeking to kill Jesus (7:1) occurs again in the dialogue we recounted in

Excavations in the city of Jerusalem. The ruins depicted here date back before the time of Jesus to Old Testament times.

verses 19–14. They were amazed at His wisdom since He didn't have a degree from the "University of Jerusalem." However, Jesus had been well taught in the synagogue schools and was Spirit-guided in what He taught and did. In fact, verses 16 and 18 give us an important key—one whose teaching seeks a glory beyond himself has the authority that is commensurate with the one he glorifies, but one who seeks his own glory has *only* his own authority.

A basic principle of learning is that we learn by obedience to the truth. We educate not only the mind, but the emotional, moral, and volitional realms of life as well. Jesus said, "If any man will do his will, he shall know of the doctrine, whether it be of God, or whether I speak of myself" (7:17). Obedience is a way of knowing. Just as in a skill-course—like playing the piano, or flying a plane—we learn by obedience in the exercises. So it is with discipleship, we learn by obedience, by decisions to follow Christ.

Verses 14–36 of John 7 may be called "the great controversy." First, Jesus' appeal to Moses was an indirect answer to their charge that He lacked formal education. In so doing He also demonstrated His skill in interpreting Moses' law. But His primary answer is that He speaks directly from God, not secondhandedly from Moses. He then argues from their own claims of accepting the authority of Moses to show them from "the law of Moses" the correctness of His gracious act of healing a man on the Sabbath (7:23). And in verse 24 Jesus concludes with the call to recognize judgment as a quality far superior to simple legalistic appearances.

Very cleverly and subtly Jesus is using His opponents' own interpretation of Moses' law for justifying His actions of doing good on the Sabbath day. And He condemns them for their inconsistency in attacking Him. Again, it is easy for us today to be critical of those who condemned Jesus' words and actions then. But each generation of Christians, including ours, is beset by legalists who fanatically pursue their own particular letter of the law and lose the Spirit of Jesus Christ.

The focus now moves to the question of Messiahship, for Jesus' references to coming from God and His authority to interpret Moses' law are Messianic. As the people try to dismiss Jesus by claiming to know His origin (7:27), He again affirms His relation to the Father, "I know him: for I am from him, and he hath sent me" (7:29). In the face of the threat of arrest, John echoes Jesus' earlier words that "His hour had not yet come."

In the next paragraph (7:32–36), Jesus confronts the arresting officers sent by the chief priests, and predicts in a parable His coming death and departure (7:33–34), leaving them perplexed. We cannot read this without being impressed with the boldness with which He taught in the temple and stood toe-to-toe with His opponents. We know from Jesus' example that when we live daily in the presence of God we need not fear any person or circumstance.

The need for open minds to recognize God's truth comes through clearly in this part of our lesson as we study the contrasts between the criticisms of Jesus by those opposed to Him and His answers and actions. He is accused of working in secret (7:4) and yet He teaches openly (7:26). Jesus is charged with leading people astray (7:12), but He responds by asserting that His teaching comes from God (7:16–18). He is denounced for having never studied (7:15), but He says boldly that His teaching is not His own but God's (7:16). They accuse Him of being demon-possessed (7:20), but throughout His teaching He honors the Father and states so specifically later in this lesson (8:49). And His origins are questioned (7:27), but He responds by declaring that He comes from God (7:29).

Now, as in Jesus' day, only persons who are open to God and are free from prejudice are able to hear His truth.

Freedom—To Have Faith.

The Festival of Tabernacles was the third of three great Jewish Festivals: Passover, Pentecost, and Tabernacles.

While observing the Festival of Tabernacles the people left their houses and lived in booths constructed with branches from palm or myrtle, and with a thatched roof as reminders of their wilderness wanderings. It was a season of gladness—a time of celebration because the harvest had been gathered (Ex. 23:16). On the last day of the festival the people would march around the altar, and one of the priests would take a quart-sized golden pitcher to the pool of Siloam, fill it with water, and carry it to the temple where it was poured on the altar as an offering to God. The people would then sing the Hallel (Psa. 113–118) to the accompaniment of a flute and recite the words of Isaiah, "With joy shall ye draw water out of the wells of salvation" (12:3).

It was in this setting that Jesus stood and cried out, "If any man thirst, let him come unto me, and drink. He that believeth on me, as the scripture hath said, out of his belly shall flow rivers of living water "(7:37–38). Jesus is the true water of life.

This reminds us of Jesus' words to the Samaritan woman, "...the water that I shall give shall be in him a well of water springing up into everlasting life" (John 4:14). At the same time Jesus may have been referring to Isaiah's words, "And the Lord shall guide thee continually, and satisfy thy soul in drought, and make fat thy bones: and thou shalt be like a watered garden, and like a spring of water, whose waters fail not" (Isa. 58:11). It is very likely that Jesus' listeners would have connected the Isaiah passage with His words.

John interprets parenthetically for us, "But this spake he of the Spirit, which they that believe on him should receive: for the Holy Ghost was not yet given; because that Jesus was not yet glorified" (7:39).

Jesus is the One who gives us the Holy Spirit—the Divine Presence—to those who believe in Him. We should note that John relates the gift of the Spirit to the glorification of Christ. The first real act of the risen Lord was to give the Holy Spirit to His disciples.

We now read that "there was a division among the people because of him" (7:43). Some said He was a prophet; others said He was the Christ, But His detractors argued that the Messiah would come from Bethlehem, not from Galilee (7:40-42). And still others wanted to get Him out of the way, to arrest Him (7:44). No one was neutral then, and we can't be neutral now—we either accept or reject Jesus. We have rejected Jesus in our time by our acceptance of a secular and materialistic way of life. Like the religious leaders of Jesus' day, we often reject Him when His teaching goes against what we want. But faith calls us to identify with Him, to follow Him.

The statement of the arresting officers when they came back to the chief priests empty-handed was a remarkable affirmation of Jesus, "Never man spake like this man" (7:46). Jesus is the Logos, the Word of God, and His words are the authoritative declarations of God. No spokesman other than Jesus could say "I am the bread of life," or "He that hath seen me hath seen the Father."

Nicodemus, whose dawning faith led him to talk with Jesus (John 3:1–18), now speaks a word in His defense (7:51). But they taunted Nicodemus, and asserted that no prophet ever came from Galilee (7:52). But they were wrong about that even as they were blinded to truth, for Jonah had come from Gath-hepher, just seven miles from Nazareth in Galilee (2 Kings 14:25).

Freedom to believe comes only as we are open to the truth of God that is above and beyond ourselves. To believe God we must look beyond what we tend to idolize as god.

We come now in our lesson to a unique and moving story (8:1–11). In it we find a marvelous expression of Jesus' spirit of grace. The setting is in the temple and it is early morning. Jesus is there "and all the people came unto him; and he sat down, and taught them" (8:2). Once

Freedom—in Forgiving Grace.

again the scribes and Pharisees enter the scene, and they had with them "a woman taken in adultery, in the very act" (8:4). A trap was being laid for Jesus by tricky scribes and Pharisees who wanted to catch Him in a bind between Roman law and Moses' law. For example, if Jesus didn't agree that this adulteress should be stoned, He would be violating Moses' law (Lev. 20:10). On the other hand, if He sanctioned her execution, He would be usurping the power of Rome. According to tradition, the procedure of Roman criminal law was to write down the sentence on a tablet and read it. So in essence Jesus said, "If you are asking me to usurp the functions of Rome, very well," and He stooped down, and with His finger wrote on the ground (8:6). John then says that "when they continued asking him, he lifted up himself and said unto them, He that is without sin among you, let him first cast a stone at her" (8:7).

What a master stroke on Jesus' part! By responding as He did Jesus showed how mercy enriches justice. That is not to say that mercy excuses sin—it holds us responsible, for Jesus said to the woman after her accusers had left, "Neither do I condemn thee: go and sin no more" (8:11).

We have no way of knowing what happened to this woman after her dramatic confrontation with Jesus. But we do know that when we are open to His love and forgiveness, we are never the same again. To experience Jesus is to experience new life. And to really know Jesus should free us from a judgmental and condemning spirit toward others.

It is likely this next scene in which Jesus continues His dialogue with the Pharisees was in the temple treasury, located in what was known as the Court of the Women. This court was the setting for a massive display of candles which were lighted during a certain part of the celebration of the Festival of Tabernacles. It was in this brilliant setting that Jesus declared boldly, "I am the light of the world: he that followeth me shall not walk in darkness, but shall have the light of life" (8:12). By this reference Jesus continued His identification as the Messianic answer to the symbolism of their pageant—the living water, and the light of life. You will recall that very early in John's Gospel, the Word—the Logos—is spoken of as "the light of men" (1:4).

The arguments in the verses following reveal a lot about Jesus as a Person. 1) He states that His witness is true because He has come from God (8:14); 2) His judgment is true because He speaks for the Father who sent Him (8:15–

16); 3) His assurance is masterful, for He points out that in their law two witnesses are required for truth—He serves as one witness, and His Father, invisible but present in the miracle-signs, is the second Witness (8:17–18). Then in response to the question, "Where is thy father?" Jesus says that the Father is revealed in His very person, "If ye had known me, ye should have known my Father also" (8:19). Through their bigotry and spiritual blindness they failed to recognize their Messiah as coming from the Father.

John adds a note in verse 20 that gives us insight into Jesus' bravery at that moment. His enemies, the Sanhedrin, were looking for an opportunity to kill Him. Yet He was teaching boldly "in the treasury," practically next door to the chamber where the Sanhedrin met.

My friend, John Perkins, tells how he was beaten severely at Brandon, Mississippi, on February 7, 1970, because he was active in the Civil Rights movement. He left Mississippi and moved to California where he was converted to Christ through the witness of his son who had begun attending Sunday school. After John's conversion he returned to Mississippi to begin the now well-known "Voice of Calvary" ministries among the people there who had suffered so much.

We learn from Jesus' boldness in declaring who He was within a few feet of His enemies' headquarters, and from John Perkins' boldness in returning to Mississippi, that when we truly know God's purpose, there is no need to run from adversity.

Freedom—in Believing Him.

We move now into a further exchange between Jesus and the Pharisees (8:21–30) that reaches its climax in verse 30, "As he spake these words, many believed on him." While other religions reach blindly in the darkness in an effort to find God, Christianity is the Word of God come to us, reaching down to us, and laying hold on us. Christianity is not a religion *we* hold, but it is God laying hold on us, calling us by His grace.

Jesus said that He came from above. In contrast, while we are all of this world, He is not of this world (8:23). And the only way to know the Father, to know forgiveness of sin, is to know His grace in Christ. The King James Version expresses His words, "...if ye believe not that I am he, ye shall die in your sins" (8:24). This is the first of three "if" statements in John 8. The second is found in verse 31 and

61

refers to our obedience as disciples. And the third is in verse 36 which speaks to our freedom in Christ.

The references to His coming death reveal that Jesus understood the direction of His life (8:21, 28). He knew full well the cost involved in following the will of the Father.

When Jesus, in referring to His death in verse 21, said that He would be leaving and His Jewish critics couldn't follow Him, they speculated cynically—hopefully—that He was talking about committing suicide. For the Jew this was a supreme sin that was punished with a special place in hell. So consumed were they in their derision of Jesus that they gave no attention to His warning about dying in their sin (8:21). The point Jesus was making was simply this: To reject Jesus Christ as Saviour and Lord separates a person from God. And this applies equally to us today as it did to the Jews who were listening to Him in the temple.

Of special significance in this passage is the direct relation between Jesus and the Father. He *spoke* from the Father (8:26). He *acted* on the authority of the Father (8:28). He *lived* in the presence of the Father (8:29a). And for His highest claim as to life-style, Jesus said, "I do always those things that please him" (8:29).

One of the unique theological aspects of these verses is Jesus' identification with God by the use of the phrase "I AM"—"I am he..." (8:24, 28). Jesus uses the expression *ego eimi*, the "I Am"—the very presence of God. This is reminiscent of Moses' meeting God at the burning bush in the wilderness when God identified Himself as "I Am."

As disciples of Christ, we come to His word with our minds already made up to obey Him. We are called to live by His authority. And we are also called to live and act in ways that please Him. Our actions and attitudes are centered in Christ. We are saved in relation to Jesus and we behave according to our relationship with Jesus. All of life is new in and through Him.

One night, in 1741, George Frederick Handel shuffled down a London street, crying, "My God, my God, why...?" When he returned to his shabby lodging, he found a package on his desk. He tore off the wrappings and found the lyrics to "A Sacred Oratorio." Also in the package was a note from Charles Jennens asking him to write the music.

Handel read listlessly until he came to the passage, "He was despised..." As he read those words, an old fire was rekindled in his soul, and grasping a pen, he began to fill sheet after sheet with his composition. When the house boy brought breakfast, he just looked past him and continued his work. At times he walked up and down shouting "Hallelujah." At last, finished with the Oratorio, he fell on the bed and slept for seventeen hours. The greatest oratorio ever written was completed, but through it Handel was reborn—he received a new freedom in Jesus Christ.

Freedom—in Belonging to God.

The Christian life is one of discipleship. Jesus calls us to come follow Him, to identify totally with Him. This means that discipleship begins with faith in Christ, it progresses by obeying His word, and it enjoys the freedom of His truth (8:31–32). In fact, it is in these verses that we find what could be called Jesus' great Declaration of Freedom... "ye shall know the truth, and *the truth shall set you free."* (italics mine). To understand as best we can what Jesus said here will cause us to shout, "Hallelujah," as Handel did in his oratorio.

Jesus' reference to freedom touched a tender spot in His hearers. They were proud of being children of Abraham, and believed they were free in their heritage (8:33). But Jesus shows the deeper truth that all people are slaves to sin until they are set free in the freedom of Christ and belong to God (8:31–47).

Jesus' statement, "If the Son therefore shall make you free, ye shall be free indeed" (8:36) is the key to understanding salvation. Jesus Christ releases us from the bondage and perversions of selfishness and frees us so that we can do the will of God. The freedom of the Son is freedom to be honest and consistent in our words and in our behavior.

The Jews had defended themselves and their actions by claiming to be Abraham's descendants. But Jesus contrasts their behavior with that of the great patriarch saying that true children of Abraham would act in the faith of Abraham. After all, he had welcomed God's messengers when they visited him on the plains of Mamre (Gen. 18), while the Jews of Jesus' day refused to receive Him.

In response to Jesus' perceptive comparison, the Jews now made the bold claim of being children of God (8:41). Their claim is to a valid heredity, "We be not born of fornication." Some interpreters consider these words a derogatory allusion to Jesus' own birth, but I don't believe the passage actually suggests this. Instead, it may well have been a self-righteous defense. But Jesus counters their claim to having God as their Father by saying that if God was indeed their Father they would accept and love Him (8:42–43). And He then pointedly declared them to be children of their father the devil (8:44).

In telling the unbelieving Jews that the devil was their father, Jesus gives us a vivid description of the nature of the devil. The devil is a murderer and a liar, and those who do his works participate in his deeds. Also, he is the source of deceit and destructive acts. By contrast, the creative love of God enables us to support and serve others for their fulfillment.

Jesus had given them a clear word about His special relationship with God when He said, "I proceeded forth and came from God; neither came I of myself, but he sent me" (8:42). Now He contrasts this fact with Satan and his lies and puts Himself on the line by asking, "Which of you convinceth me of sin" (8:46). And then Jesus makes the decisive statement that people either hear or don't hear based on whether or not they are identifying with God (8:47). And to drive the point home Jesus flatly asserts they "are not of God."

The question is not, first, do we understand God? Rather, it is, do we want God in our lives! If we want to know God and want to walk with Him, we will hear His Word.

Not everyone who observes the acts of God either understands or identifies with Him. Instead many people attempt to support God's word of grace with their own structures of religion. The famous architect, Sir Christopher Wren, designed the interior of Windsor Town Hall near London in 1689 with the ceiling supported only by the pillars in the outer walls. When the city fathers inspected the finished building, they decided that the ceiling would not stay up so they ordered Wren to put in more pillars. Wren disagreed with their conclusion but knew he had to satisfy them so he created an optical illusion by adding four pillars that didn't reach the ceiling.

While God does not deal in illusions, the pillars we would add to His grace are useless.

Freedom—to Hear Jesus.

The Jews Jesus had been talking to were enraged when He told them they "were not of God." This was a stinging rebuke for people who took pride in their religious heritage. So they lashed out at Him by accusing Him of being a Samaritan, a half-breed—not a good Jew. And they capped that derisive insult by accusing Him of being demon-possessed (8:48). But Jesus responds calmly that He honors the Father while they dishonor Him with their unbelief.

Next Jesus makes the amazing claim that if a person "keep my saying, he shall never see death" (8:51). From this we understand that one who knows God goes from life to life—from this life to the presence of God. Now Jesus' listeners were outraged even further, and they refer again to Abraham, who is dead, and the prophets who are also dead. Then they said in effect, "Who do you claim to be?" (8:53).

Again Jesus' answers calmly but firmly that He honors and glorifies the Father and the Father honors Him. The personal relationship with which Jesus refers to God is a revelation that we aren't to think of God as an idea or a universal principle or only as a source of being—He is a personal, knowable God. Simply stated, Jesus speaks of knowing Him and keeping His word (8:55).

Jesus then concludes this bit of dialogue with another of His great claims: He is the eternal Word, "Before Abraham was, I am" (8:58). This, again, is a deliberate identification with the God (Yahweh) who said to Moses, "I AM THAT I AM" (Ex. 3:14). There is only One who can say "I AM," and that One is God.

Jesus sets His claims and revelation in the context of salvation history. All that God has done in the past has involved His Logos, His Word. And persons of faith have been those whose vision of God enabled them to see His person and His work. This accounts for the fact that Jesus was able to say that Abraham had actually seen the Messianic age to come (8:56). Their claim to be Abraham's seed (8:37) was now brought to the ultimate test—could they in the spirit of Abraham recognize the Messiah?

John's reference to the Jews taking up stones to stone Jesus reveals their reaction to Him (8:59). They were closed to hearing Him as Truth and so they judged Him as a blasphemer.

We must also say that either Jesus was who He claimed to be, or He was a mad man! The more we understand of Jesus the more convinced we become that He was and is the one authentic person the world has ever seen. The question Jews asked Jesus, "Whom makest thou thyself?"—who do you claim to be?—is still being asked today. And the answer is the same now as it was then.

The story of Signor Antonio of Minas, Brazil was released by the American Bible Society. Someone gave him a Bible. He vowed to burn it, and upon returning home he kindled a fire. In order to make it burn better, he opened it. But the Bible never landed in the fire because his eyes picked out a few lines from Jesus' Sermon on the Mount. Arrested by its message, he read on further and became so engrossed that he read all night. As dawn was breaking, he stood up and declared, "I believe!" He heard Jesus and found the freedom to believe.

Freedom—to See!   In one sense, this part of our lesson (9:1–41) might be called "Freedom to be!" Here we have an encounter between a man who had been born blind and Jesus. Next John tells us that the disciples asked a penetrating question, "Master, who did sin, this man or his parents, that he was born blind?" (9:2).

The question assumes a direct relationship between sin and suffering, as was taught by the Rabbis. Jesus dismissed the relationship between sin and suffering by placing His emphasis on the presence and creative work of God in the human situation (9:3).

We learn an important truth from these words of Jesus—ours is a precarious world in which accidents happen. But the Good News of the gospel is that we can invite the work of God into our difficulties and into the perversions of life.

Jesus' emphasis here is on the "Light of Life" that is come into the world, as He states boldly, "I am the light of the world" (9:5). And the function of light is to expel darkness.

As disciples of Christ we, too, are light in the world, "punching holes in the darkness."

Then as a sign of this claim to be "the light of the world," Jesus healed the blind man. Jesus' emphasis on the work of God (9:4) tells us that social concern and the proclamation of the Good News are companion expressions of grace. When we work to help others who are in need, we are manifesting the glory of God in our world today and are giving a positive expression of what God is like.

This sixth miracle-sign—the healing of the blind man occurred on the Sabbath, the day of rest and release. But the

Jewish leaders were so legalistic about the details of "rest," of no work, that they missed the personal wholeness the Sabbath was intended to provide. Jesus' act of making clay and anointing the man's eyes (9:6) was interpreted as "work," as violating their Sabbath laws. Because of this the joy of the man's healing was lost in their censorious spirit of religious intolerance. It is said that someone once asked Friedrich Nietzsche, the German atheistic philosopher, why he was negative toward the Christian faith. His reply was a serious indictment against Christians of his time and ours, "I was never impressed that the members of my father's church enjoyed their religion." What a tragedy! And how contrary to the spirit of Jesus!

Jesus' emphasis on being the light of the world is evidently reason enough for John to include the entire story of the continuing dialogue between the Jewish leaders and the healed man (9:13–18) and his parents (9:19–25). The dialogue shows the growth of faith insight in the restored man and the darkness of unbelief in the members of the Sanhedrin. As they closed their minds to the truth, their only recourse was to try to confront truth with power. They excommunicated the man (9:34).

Significantly, the parents of the man had refused to speak up for the truth because they feared being excommunicated (9:22–23). But the man who had been healed, who had been touched by God, could not help but witness to the reality of his encounter with Jesus! This is the contrast between prejudice and conviction, the conflict between the raw power of force and the spiritual power of truth.

The actions of the Sanhedrin in response to the miracle is threefold. First, they examined the blind man to hear His story. Second, they examined the parents to confirm the story. And third, they re-examined and excommunicated the man who had been healed of his blindness.

In the examination of the man who had been blind, a division arose among his inquisitors because some of them recognized from what had happened that Jesus was a Prophet of God (9:16). When the parents were examined, they copped out to save their necks. And in the examination of the healed man, we hear him begin to witness as a disciple of Jesus! His response to the Sanhedrin is classic, "...one thing I know, that whereas I was blind, now I see" (9:25). The old adage stands, "A man with an experience is never at the mercy of a man with an argument!"

A poet and an artist were looking at a painting by the French master, Nicolas Poussin, of the healing of the blind man at Jericho, another miracle related in the Gospels. The artist asked the poet what he thought was the most impressive thing in the painting. The poet complimented the expressions on the faces, but the artist shook his head and pointed to a discarded cane on the steps of a house, "there is the evidence of faith."

The final movement in this remarkable story of healing occurred when Jesus looked for the man after he had been excommunicated, and identified with him (9:35–38). Chrysostom, in commenting on this story, said, "The Jews cast him out of the temple; the Lord of the temple found him."

The Jews had said that anyone who confessed Jesus as the Messiah would be excommunicated from the fellowship of Israel (9:22). Now Jesus turns the tables on them (9:39–41) by announcing the judgment implicit in His presence, for in the rejection of the truth of Jesus, the blindness of the Jews remained.

Our freedom in Christ comes when we *see* Him as our Lord and Saviour in every part of our lives—in the home, on the street, and in the marketplaces of our world.

Lord, Thank You for being my teacher, my strength, my help, and the "lifter up of my head." AMEN.

WHAT THIS SCRIPTURE MEANS TO ME—John 7–9

Three intensely moving stories leap out at me from this particular Scripture lesson. Each focuses on Jesus in a unique and different way as He moves into the last months of His earthly life.

Jesus is home in Galilee. This is familiar ground—the rolling hills around Nazareth, the lakeshore with its bustling fishing towns—Tiberias, Bethsaida, and Capernaum. From childhood He had known this country well. And many of the faces were familiar. Here were friends, neighbors, and even His family.

But this was a sad time, for there were those who wanted to kill Him. And even His own brothers didn't believe in Him. They sarcastically derided Him saying, "Why don't you go on back to Judea where your disciples can see what you are doing and be impressed? Nobody is seeing what you are doing here, and we don't have any faith in you." Such cruel words must have cut Jesus deeply, but He calmly urged His brothers to go on to Jerusalem without Him to celebrate the Jewish festival. Then after they had gone, He traveled south alone and covertly entered the city.

Assuming He would attend the festival in Jerusalem the Jews there kept looking for Him for there was an undercurrent of discussion about Him among the crowds.

"Where is that man?"

"He is a good man."

"No He's not. He is misleading the people."

Then later when Jesus moved out into the open, He asked the crowd in the temple, "Why are you trying to kill me?" They answered him, "Surely you must be mad! Who is trying to kill you?"

But the Pharisees *were* trying to kill him. In fact, they had sent officers to arrest Him. And when the officers returned without Jesus, they were asked, "Why haven't you brought him?" Their reply was more prophetic than they knew, "No man ever spoke as this man speaks."

There's an intriguing subplot in this story. While the carping crowd of Jesus' critics was nipping and snapping at Him like cornered animals, Nicodemus came to His defense. Apparently Nicodemus had been following Jesus at every opportunity since that night when he had questioned Him about the new birth (John 3:1–21). But when Nicodemus defended Jesus, the Pharisees turned on him and shouted, "Are you a Galilean too?"

"Look where you will," they railed. "You won't find any prophet coming out of Galilee." How wrong they were! For Elijah, Elisha, Jonah, Hosea, Naham, and Amos came out of Galilee—and that's an impressive list.

This event reminds me that if we are truly disciples of Jesus and His Holy Spirit dwells in us, we can expect at times to be ridiculed and misunderstood even as Jesus was. But for each of us there may be a "Nicodemus" watching what is going on. And what a joy it will be either here or in the hereafter for someone to say, "It was you who invited me to become a follower of the Master."

The second story is about the woman caught in adultery. The Pharisees brought her to Jesus not to do justice but to try to trap Him. This was a part of their diabolical plan to get Him to say or do something they could legally use against Him.

After Jesus wrote their sins in the ground they slipped away like the guilty men that they were. But listen to the dialogue.

"Where are they all—did no one condemn you?"

"No one, Lord."

"Neither do I condemn you. Go away now and do not sin again."

Recently I asked my new friend Jo to go to church with us, but when we went by for her, she wasn't at home.

The next day I asked her what happened. Why had she stood us up?

"Oh, I'm sorry," she replied. "Really I am. It's just that I can't take all those 'drop dead' looks that I always get from most church people."

Jesus forgave the woman in this story, and He is ready to forgive Jo. But His judgment on the Pharisees was harsh. I wonder if church people who deliver "drop dead" looks are not equally guilty. Jesus is still saying, "Let him who is without sin cast the first stone."

In the closing scene of this lesson we see Jesus heal an unnamed man who had been blind since birth. After the blind man's encounter with Jesus, he had 20-20 spiritual vision as well as physical sight. But the querulous Pharisees who had visual eyesight were blind spiritually, and Jesus condemned them for their self-righteous attitude.

We have a friend who was blinded in an oil field injury many years ago. His senses of smell and touch and hearing are much more acute than mine. So is his spiritual perception.

We have another friend who is a plastic surgeon. His patients almost worship him. He has fame and money and the croupiers in Las Vegas all know him by name, but he feels no need for God.

Jesus said to the blind man in Jerusalem that day, "I am the light of the world." Our sightless friend has experienced that light. It is our daily hope and prayer that our surgeon friend will become aware of his blindness.

The great good news for us is that Jesus will meet our needs and enrich our lives as our eyes are open to Him.

LESSON 4
JOHN 10–12

Christ the Reconciler—in Truth

Gracious Father, Sanctify me through Your truth: Your Word is truth. AMEN.

Truth is a unified whole, not just a collection of ideas. Paul, though, was very specific when he wrote to the Ephesians, "…the truth is in Jesus" (Eph. 4:21). And Jesus Himself said, "I am the way, the truth and the life" (John 14:6).

Truth is personified in Jesus. He is the truth about God, the truth about genuine humanness. Jesus is the truth about divine grace…about salvation…about the Kingdom of God…about life and destiny. As John wrote in the opening verses of the Gospel, "The law was given by Moses, but grace and truth came by Jesus Christ" (1:17).

One of our prized possessions is an oil painting by Anton Mauve, the nineteenth-century Mennonite artist. It is a picture of a shepherd carrying a lamb as he walks among his sheep and talks to them while they move along under his patient leadership.

Truth—as the Good Shepherd.

A shepherd tending a flock of sheep was a familiar sight in first-century Palestine. So Jesus now uses this imagery to get across the idea that He is the Good Shepherd (10:11, 14) and His sheep follow Him because they know and recognize His voice (10:4–5). It was common practice in those days for shepherds to let their flocks intermingle. But with just a few words from their shepherd, the sheep would

The Good Shepherd leads the sheep with care and concern. Here we have a view of a modern shepherd leading his sheep through some recently harvested grain fields.

move apart from the others and follow the familiar voice.

The occasion for the parable (10:1–5) immediately follows the confrontation with the Pharisees over their spiritual blindness (9:40–41). Now as they listened to Jesus' words, they doubtless recalled the Old Testament references to God as the Shepherd of Israel (Psa. 80:1) and as Shepherd for His people (Psa. 23). Building on the imagery of the Psalmist, they identified themselves as being the sheep of His pasture (Psa. 95:7; 100:3; 79:13). The words of Isaiah (40:11) and Ezekiel (34:23) would also come to mind, identifying the Messiah as the Shepherd.

At the same time they would have remembered in those

prophetic passages the condemnation of false shepherds. And so we find in Jesus' story here a denunciation of false shepherds while affirming His own unique role as the Good Shepherd.

There are three pictures of Jesus presented in these verses: "I am the door" of the sheepfold (10:9); "I am the good shepherd" (10:11); and "I lay down my life" as the sacrificial lamb (10:17–18).

As the door to the sheepfold, He is the entry into the fellowship of the people of God, the way into salvation (10:9). It is only through Jesus that we are able to find God—He alone is the door; He is our security. And then after asserting His role Jesus expresses the superlative character of His own mission, "I am come that they might have life, and that they might have it more abundantly" (10:10). Life in Christ is the expanding life; it is life enriched by *all* of the resources found in fellowship with God! In contrast to the 20,000 priests serving in the temple and some 7,000 Pharisees who served as teachers, Jesus stood alone as the doorway to life and to God.

The second picture is of Jesus as the Good Shepherd who 1) gives His life for the sheep—He puts us first (10:11, 15); 2) He knows His sheep (10:14)—He identifies with us and cares for us; 3) He extends His mission to those beyond the ethnic boundaries of Israel (10:16)—He cares for all; and 4) He brings together all who hear His voice (10:16).

The voluntary nature of Jesus' coming sacrificial death is expressed in verses 17–18. Jesus knew that He would give His life in obedience to the Father's will—it would be no accident but rather an achievement. He would fulfill the nature of God's love in giving Himself to redeem humanity once and for all (John 3:16).

In this passage Jesus not only expressed the voluntary aspect of His coming death, but He also affirmed the victorious faith with which He anticipated death—He knew that at God's command He would be raised up again (10:18). And in Jesus Christ we share in that same faith as we face death, for Jesus promised to raise us up "at the last day" (6:54).

Once again John points to the division among the people because of Jesus (10:19–21). Some argued that He was insane and others said He was devil-possessed. But then there were those who said His words and actions were not those of a mad or demon-possessed man. Then and now—

and throughout all intervening time—people are brought to a place of decision when confronted by Jesus Christ. We are either for Him or against Him. We either take God seriously or insult Him by indifference. And indifference is the ultimate insult—the opposite of love.

Truth—the Exposing of Unbelief.

We are told now that the words and events in this part of our lesson (10:22–42) occurred during the Festival of Dedication. Its Jewish name is Hanukkah, and it was founded to commemorate the victory of Judas Maccabee over the Syrians and the rededication of the temple in 165 B.C. It was winter, John tells us, the 25th of the Jewish month that parallels our month of December. The setting for this next bit of dialogue was "in the temple in Solomon's porch." Again a crowd gathered around Jesus and asked a penetrating question, "How long dost thou make us to doubt? If thou be the Christ, tell us plainly" (10:24). His answer was to give them evidence by pointing to the works He had done in His Father's name. As Chrysostom, a fourth-century Christian leader, paraphrased, "If ye follow me not, it is not because I am not a shepherd, but because ye are not my sheep." Jesus knew their question wasn't honest but was intended to entrap Him.

He knew they wouldn't understand Him because they weren't "His Sheep." And then He goes on to tell about 1) the character of His sheep—they follow Him (10:27); 2) the salvation of His sheep—they are given eternal life (10:28); and 3) the security of His sheep (10:28b–29)—"and no man is able to pluck them out of my Father's hand."

In these electrifying words Jesus is telling us that no power can overcome the Father, no one can come between us and Him. Paul expressed this in the marvelous words of Romans 8:38–39, "For I am persuaded, that neither death, nor life, nor angels, nor principalities, nor powers, nor things present, nor things to come, nor height, nor depth, nor any other creature, shall be able to separate us from the love of God, which is in Christ Jesus our Lord." Only the human will, in the freedom of our own choice, can say "no" to God. Our security is that in saying "yes" to God we are secure in Him. Jude writes, "...building up yourselves on your most holy faith, praying in the Holy Ghost, keep yourselves in the love of God..." (verses 20–21a).

The statement "I and my Father are one" (10:30) expresses the unity of will and purpose between Jesus and the Father. But this claim to oneness with God was heard by the Jews as blasphemy, and they took up stones to kill Him. Before they could act, though, Jesus took the initiative and asked, "Many good works have I shewed you from my Father; for which of those works do ye stone me?" (10:32). Their answer tells us that even though they had heard His claim, they refused to accept it, "For a good work we stone thee not; but for blasphemy; and because that thou, being a man, makest thyself God" (11:53). They had asked Him to declare whether or not He was the Messiah. Jesus had responded by saying, "I and my Father are one"—but they refused to believe.

Jesus next reveals His wisdom and the shrewdness of His ability to argue with them (10:34–38). His appeal to their law enabled Him to declare His Messiahship—the Father had sent Him into the world (10:36), and He was right in claiming to be the Son of God (10:37–38). Jesus' words and His works were in agreement! Here is our model for all times as disciples of Christ—our words and our services of compassion confirm each other in the witness of the gospel.

John now tells us how intense their unbelief and hostility had become. Theirs was not a passive indifference but an active disbelief, a rejection, because He was an affront to their own position (10:39). John next tells us that Jesus escaped and traveled from Jerusalem down to the Jordan valley and across to Peraea, east of the Jordon River (10:40). This movement of Jesus emphasizes just how critical and dangerous the situation was. It is possible that in going to the region where John the Baptist had baptized Him and had designated Him as the "Lamb of God" was a deliberate choice—an identification with John's Messianic announcements.

We read in verses 40 and 41 that many of the people of this region believed on Jesus. The extent of their belief is expressed in words I would like as an epitaph—John "did no miracle, but all things that John spake of this man were true" (11:41).

Jesus knew, of course, what was ahead for Him. We've seen Him in this scene as He returned to the place where His ministry had started some three years before. His witness to His Father's message of salvation was clear and many believed. In this, we see our own mission for today. Ours is an insecure and threatening world, but we, too, are called to be faithful in our witness for Christ by words and actions in every part of our lives.

Truth—Discerning Divine Purpose.

The truth about life is more than the natural mind can understand. Life is not bordered by the cradle and the grave. Billions of years from now we can be living on with God! This is resurrection hope, resurrection faith. We are not just persons with immortal souls, but persons made in God's image, who are to be resurrected for life beyond time as we know it.

The story of the raising of Lazarus (11:1–16) gives us the seventh sign in the Gospel of John. Revealed in this event is the truth about life, about God's purpose of sharing the larger dimension of life with us. And the way in which Jesus postponed going to Bethany after hearing that His friend Lazarus was sick can only be understood by assuming that He was fully aware of the divine purpose in this.

John identifies Lazarus as the brother of Martha and Mary. Luke writes about the sisters but doesn't tell us about their brother (Luke 10:38–42). And here, in verse 2, we are told that Mary is the one who anointed Jesus' feet, but John drops this in as identification while that story is told later in 12:1–9.

Jesus apparently frequented this home in Bethany, a small hillside village just two miles or so from Jerusalem. In fact, it is quite likely that some of the time this was His "home away from home" when He was teaching and ministering in Jerusalem. Their friendship was a close one, so it was quite natural for Mary and Martha to send word to Jesus about their brother, "...he whom thou lovest is sick" (11:3). And in verse 5 the Gospel writer expands on Jesus' relationship with this tightly knit family as he adds, "Now Jesus *loved* Martha and her sister, and Lazarus" (italics mine).

Jesus' response, as He shared the news with His disciples, was to develop a progressive awareness of Lazarus's plight. First, He said, "This sickness is not unto death" (11:4). Next He said, "Our friend Lazarus sleepeth" (11:11), and finally He announced, "Lazarus is dead" (11:14). However, from the beginning Jesus affirmed that the illness of Lazarus was "...for the glory of God, that the Son of God might be glorified thereby" (11:4). And the glory of the Son of God *is His power over death*. It is this assurance that accounts for His announcements of His coming death without fear.

John now tells us that Jesus stayed on where He was for two more days before announcing, "Let us go into Judea again" (11:7). It was quite understandable that this word disturbed the disciples. They had left Judea for the country east of the Jordan River because of the threats on Jesus' life. Now, He was going back into that hotbed of opposition! But He reminds His disciples that a day has twelve hours, a declaration that God's purpose will be fulfilled in the proper time—a day doesn't end before those purposes are completed, and our work is in the day when it is light, not in the night. Here Jesus' word picture moves to references to the light of the world, a metaphor that directs our minds to Christ Himself.

It is then that Jesus tells His disciples, "Our friend Lazarus sleepeth; but I go, that I may awake him out of sleep" (11:11). And when the disciples still didn't understand (11:12), He announced bluntly, "Lazarus is dead."

God's intention is made clear in verse 15, where Jesus says that the purpose of the whole event is to enhance the disciples' faith. But they failed to understand this dimension of faith before the event. Faith is response to evidence, and that would come later at the tomb of Lazarus.

While the disciples lacked this dimension of faith, they had faith in Jesus, even if it meant death! Thomas summed up their feelings when he said, "Let us also go, that we may die with him" (11:16). Thomas' words tell us that the disciples were fully aware of the violent hostility the Jewish religious leaders had toward Jesus. They also remind us of Peter's words some days later, that he would die with Christ (Matt. 26:35), and yet at the crucial moment in the courtyard of the high priest he denied Him.

This certainly serves to illustrate the truth from Jeremiah, "The heart is deceitful above all things and desperately wicked: who can know it" (Jer. 17:9). The answer comes loud and clear through the Gospel story: God knows us and loves us anyway! He loves us, even when we are caught in what Dr. Thomas Kelley called straddled arrangements: "Sometimes I think there are two of me, a living soul and a Ph.D."

Truth—as
Resurrection Power.

There is a power greater than death, the power of life! And Jesus came to reconcile us with life. "I am come that ye might have life, and have it more abundantly" (10:10). The miracle of raising Lazarus was a sign to everyone of the truth of Jesus' words, "I am the resurrection, and the life: he that believeth in me, though he were dead, yet shall he live" (11:25).

We turn our attention now to one of the most dramatic stories in the entire Gospel account (11:17–46). In studying these verses I want us to look at the four divisions in its development: 1) Jesus' conversation about the resurrection; 2) Jesus' deep emotion in the face of death; 3) Jesus' call that awakes the dead; 4) Jesus is totally rejected by the religious leaders.

In the other Gospels there are accounts of Jesus raising people from the dead—Jarius' daughter (Matt. 9:18–26) and the widow's son at Nain (Luke 7:11–16). In both of these cases life was restored soon after death, and there could have been those who interpreted them as resuscitation. But Lazarus had been *dead* four days! Here, without question, was a full witness to resurrection power.

Jesus' conversation with Martha (11:20–28), is a most significant treatment of resurrection. There was no uniform or common belief among the Jewish parties about life after physical death. On one hand, the Sadducees did not believe in the resurrection. But the Pharisees held a strong belief in a resurrection from the dead. Undoubtedly, these conflicting beliefs had been discussed in Lazarus' home.

But let's look now at the conversation between Jesus and Martha. When He arrived on the outskirts of Bethany, she greeted Him by saying, "Lord, if thou hadst been here, my brother had not died" (11:21). It sounds very much as if she was chiding Jesus for His delay in getting there. But then her faith in the Lord took over and she added, "But I know, that even now, whatsoever thou wilt ask of God, God will give it to thee" (11:22).

Now notice Jesus' response, "Thy brother shall rise again." Martha then affirmed her belief in the resurrection—life beyond the grave (11:24). She had come to the heart of faith which could affirm the Father's promise, "I will raise him up at the last day" (6:40). The high-water mark of Old Testament hope had become clear for her;

The traditional location of Lazarus' tomb in Bethany.

she could then say with Job, "And though after my skin
worms destroy this body, yet in my flesh shall I see God:
Whom I shall see for myself, and mine eyes shall behold,
and not another..." (Job 19:26–27). Now came some of
Jesus' grandest words, "*I am the resurrection, and the life*: he

that believeth in me, though he were dead, *yet shall he live*: And whosoever liveth and believeth in me, *shall never die*" (11:25–26, italics mine).

When Martha heard those words, she made her soul-changing confession that Jesus was in truth the Messiah—the Son of God (11:27). Undoubtedly, there was more to the conversation than John wrote down, for Martha left Jesus, hurried home and said to Mary "The Master is come, and calleth for thee."

What a marvelous word in any time of difficulty—"the Master is come." To know God's compassion, His caring, is enough to transform every difficulty into a possibility. And to have the added personal word that He "calleth for thee" means that Jesus was particularly concerned about Mary—even as He is for you and me. What was Mary's response to this good news? "…she arose quickly, and came unto him" (11:29). That says it all!

In the next scene we see Jesus in the way confronted by the weeping Mary and surrounded by the attending mourners. The depth of His grief comes through in John's vivid words, "…he groaned in the spirit, and was troubled" (11:33). Jesus had lost a close friend, but more important—we catch a glimpse of how deeply He felt about death. God is not an unfeeling, distant being, but a God who shares and participates in the anguish of His people. The shortest verse in the Bible expresses the depth of God's caring, "Jesus wept" (11:35). And groaning within Himself, fully aware of the weight of His conflict with death, Jesus made His way to the cave that was Lazarus' grave (11:38).

After telling the mourners to remove the stone from the mouth of the cave, and responding to Martha's concern about the condition of her brother's body, Jesus prayed an intimate prayer to His Heavenly Father. And upon the conclusion of that short but confident prayer, Jesus shouted, "Lazarus come forth" (11:43). And then the crowd saw "the glory of God" as Lazarus shuffled out of the cave.

Jesus knew the dead could hear His voice and would respond. As the Victor over death, Jesus reached into the region of the departed and brought Lazarus back and reunited him with his sisters and friends. The reconstituting of a wasted body was a secondary miracle in relation to the primary one—Lazarus was back!

As I reflect on this scene, the hairs on my arms stand straight up in the midst of the goose bumps. I can't help but wonder what Jesus felt as He looked at His old friend. But even in the middle of this awesome scene, Jesus had the presence of mind to say, "Loose him, and let him go."

John next gives us the reaction of the crowd, "Many… believed on him" (11:45). But others, filled with self-righteous bigotry, turned their backs on what Jesus had done and carried a tale to the conniving Pharisees (11:45–46).

We have in this part of our lesson a ring of truth that we are meant to hear. God is at work in our world even today as we rush pell-mell toward the twenty-first century. Our mission is to be open—to *listen* and to *see*. If we shut out avenues of truth and people who worship God and live for Him in ways that differ from ours, we may well miss the awesome and majestic glory of God and the difference it makes in the lives of people who are pressing toward that glory.

Truth—Confronting the Powers.

Earthly power tends to idolatry. It becomes an end in itself, an ultimate. As Edmund Burke, eighteenth-century statesman and orator once said, "Power corrupts, absolute power corrupts absolutely." And power of position has a problem with the power of truth. Justice calls for equality of opportunity for all persons, but the structures of power build a pyramid and trap the people at the lower levels as servants to those at the upper levels. But such power structures are threatened when those at the lower levels are treated with equal privilege as the leaders.

In this part of our lesson now the Sanhedrin, made up of both Pharisees and Sadducees, is assembled to plan what to do about Jesus (11:47–53). His type of power, the Messianic power of redemptive love, of reconciling grace, challenged the uses of power for the dominance of one group of people by another. The threat to the Sanhedrin was seen by them as a threat to Rome, the power structure to which they answered. After all, if Jesus in any way created a public uprising or disorder, their position would be threatened. They had to get rid of Him and His reconciling power which was in sharp opposition to their self-interests.

It was my privilege to be acquainted with the Honorable Brooks Hays, U.S. Congressman from Arkansas, who opposed Governor Orval Faubes on the civil rights issue. As a consequence of Hays' defense of equal rights, he lost his bid for re-election. When news of his defeat was released, a professor from the Southern Baptist Seminary in New Orleans wired him this message, "Dear Brooks, you taught us that we gain by giving, we win by losing, and we live by dying. Congratulations on winning!"

In response to the Sanhedrin debate about Jesus, the words of Caiaphas were bold and crude, matching the pattern of the arrogant Sadducees, "Ye know nothing at all"—in so many words he was saying, "If you had any sense, You would know..." And then the high priest went on to say "that it is expedient for us, that one man should die for the people and that the whole nation perish not" (11:50). It is ironic that Caiaphas, in making this speech, was actually foretelling Jesus' vicarious death without realizing it (11:51). John interprets the words as a prophecy of Jesus' redemptive work in His death, to "gather together in one the children of God that were scattered abroad" (11:52). In other words, Jesus, in His death, would demonstrate the reconciling truth that draws everyone from the sin of self-structures to the fellowship of a gracious self-giving God.

Jesus was not reckless, and so because of the violent hostility of His enemies, He withdrew to the hills that were north of Jerusalem to Ephraim in the region of Bethel (11:54–57). But in the Jewish community Jesus was now a fugitive with a price on His head. The Sanhedrin ordered the people to report on Jesus, to tell them where He was located. The sinister conspiracy against Jesus was gaining momentum, and John now tells us that the people, who were gathering to purify themselves in the temple court in preparation for the Passover, were discussing among themselves whether Jesus would put in an appearance at the feast.

Truth—In Messianic Announcement.

John's selection of the three unique scenes of this section of our study (12:1–36) present three aspects of Jesus' reconciling work: 1) the preparation for His suffering and death; 2) the announcement of His role as King of Kings; and 3) the universal nature of His redemptive mission.

In scene one (12:1–9) Jesus has come out of seclusion and is in Bethany at the home of Lazarus. Once again Jesus is among friends who love Him, and they were enjoying dinner together on the Saturday evening before Palm Sunday as we know it. Martha, true to form, was serving dinner. Lazarus sat at the table with Jesus, and an assortment of curious Jews filled the courtyard of this wealthy home to get a look at the resurrected Lazarus, as well as at Jesus (12:9).

This church is built over the traditional home of Mary, Martha, and Lazarus. The mosaic depicts the presence of Jesus with the family, and the inscription reads, "I am the resurrection and the life."

But the main actress in this drama is Mary, the sister, who brought a pound of nard, an oriental ointment that had cost "300 denarii," a whole year's wages for a day laborer, and poured it on Jesus' feet. In an act of humble devotion she loosed her hair and wiped His feet. The aroma filled the house and everyone became aware of her gesture of love. Love has a way of enriching the whole community. Love gives its all, for Jesus' love was to give all—Himself.

John Wesley believed that holiness was social and ethical, and in his stewardship he gave most of his income to the poor. In 1776 he received a letter from the Commissioners of Excise, stating, "We cannot doubt but that you have a plate for which you have hitherto neglected to make an entry." Wesley wrote in reply, "I have two silver spoons at London and two in Bristol. This is all I have at present, and I shall not buy any more while so many around me want bread."

This scene also introduces Judas Iscariot as a negative voice (12:4–5). His crass materialism blinded him to Mary's expression of love. He counted the cost, and we learn of the extent of Mary's extravagance through his ill-mannered criticism. Judas, like most critics, attempted to cover his real motive with a good face, for he asked "Why was this ointment not sold...and given to the poor?" (12:5). But John explains that he didn't ask this out of concern for the poor but because he was a thief (12:6), and as treasurer for the group, he probably helped himself to the funds. This interpretation by the writer was possible because of the distance from the event in which the Gospel was written. The disciples were not aware of Judas's deceit until much later than the Bethany event.

Jesus responded to Judas' criticism of Mary by saying that the ministry to the poor could be fulfilled at any time, but to prepare for His death could only be done now (12:8). There is always the proper time to share love, and when the opportunity passes, it rarely comes again to any of us in the same way.

The second scene is the triumphal entry into Jerusalem (12:10–19). John injects a reference in this account to the Sanhedrin wanting to kill Lazarus to destroy the living evidence to Jesus' miracle—further proof of their violent hostility to Jesus. The primary emphasis in this scene, though, is on the courage of Jesus as He rode publicly through the crowds of Passover pilgrims into Jerusalem in the face of His enemies! That He came on the back of a lowly donkey rather than on a charging white horse speaks of the peaceful nature of the Messiah. Jesus did not ride into the city as a conquering king but as the Prince of Peace.

A view of Jerusalem from the Mount of Olives. The modern Dome of the Rock or Mosque of Omar is located on the site of the temple where Jesus taught.

This must have been a fearsome and awesome moment for Jesus' close followers. While the crowds along the road that day seemed to welcome Him, the disciples knew of the death threats that had been made against Him. But John now tells us that they didn't understand what all of this meant until after Jesus' death, resurrection, and ascension (12:16). Only then did they connect these events with the Old Testament prophesies, including Zechariah (9:9).

At the same time Jesus' enemies among the Jewish religious leaders were dumbfounded, frustrated, and furious. To them it seemed He had flaunted His presence when He openly rode into Jerusalem on that first Palm

Sunday. But they didn't dare take Him then because of the crowd's enthusiasm, "...behold, the whole world is gone after him" (12:19).

The third scene, given us only in John's Gospel, is a moving occasion that signals the interest in Jesus by the gentile world in contrast to Jewish unbelief (12:20-36). Some Greeks, possibly involved in their customary search for truth, were in Jerusalem—they may well have been looking into the worship of Jehovah. Certainly, their inquiry of Philip gives us a striking focus on worship, "Sir, we would see Jesus" (12:21). Perhaps they had been in the crowd when Jesus cleansed the Gentile Court of the temple, and now they wanted to meet Him personally. In response to their request Philip took them to his brother Andrew, and once again we focus our attention on Andrew as the one who took people to Jesus (12:22). Without doubt, Andrew is a prime model for us today as we seek to fulfill our witness.

Jesus took this opportunity to declare some important truth. In verse 23 He announces, "The hour is come, that the Son of man should be glorified." This was likely an electrifying statement to the Jews who were listening because of their traditional understanding of what it meant for the Son of Man to be glorified. They would have interpreted this as the long looked-for moment when the conquering Messiah would move across the world and subdue all their enemies. But when Jesus used the word "glorified," He was referring to His coming death on the cross.

Then, Jesus' words in verses 25 and 26 responded directly to the Greek philosophy of self-esteem that was so prevalent in the world at that time—and still is today. The Jesus way of life is that of the Suffering Servant: the seed falls into the ground and dies before it can give new life... "He that loveth his life shall lose it, and he that hateth his life in this world shall keep it unto life eternal" (12:24–25). This contrast between powers and service, between self-fulfillment and discipleship of Christ, continues to be the point of decision in faith just as much today as it did when John's Gospel was written.

While John in his Gospel does not include the picture of Jesus' agony in the Garden of Gethsemane, we do catch something of that struggle in the prayerful expression of Jesus found in verses 27 and 28. Here His servant role is responded to by a confirming voice from heaven. Jesus interpreted this as a sign of the purpose of God and of the judgment of God exposing and completely defeating the devil—"The prince of this world." And then, right in the middle of this victory passage Jesus referred to His coming death, "And I, if I be lifted up from the earth, will draw all men unto me" (12:32).

From our vantage point in history, we can look back and testify to the fact that truer words were never spoken. Jesus' words and message has touched every generation across the world since His "glorification." And this will continue to the end of time.

Jesus' final words in this section call for His listeners to walk in the light—in the truth of God. And with that, He withdrew from them and hid, leaving them to ponder the implication of the truth they had heard.

In this closing movement of our lesson (12:37–50) we confront the truth that unbelief is not passiveness; it is an active disbelief. It is a choice to reject the truth. In the face of the many miracles Jesus wrought, the unbelieving people continued to reject Him (12:37). John then quotes the prophet Isaiah to show how their unbelief did not alter God's purpose of redemption. The acts of reconciliation by a gracious God are genuine acts, not projections of Israel's "dream wish." And when the people of Israel satisfied themselves with religion rather than with God, the divine revelation was given in spite of their unbelief. Since the people didn't want God, He in turn kept them from fully understanding, lest their response of converting be a response to truths without being a desire for the Truth!

There is a significant contrast between Isaiah with his vision of God's glory (12:41), and the chief rulers who believed in God's Son but who were too concerned about their religious positions to confess Him (12:42–43). It was true then, and it is true now—when people love the praise of men more than the praise of God, they continue in unbelief. Earlier, Jesus had spoken to this fatal flaw when He said, "How can ye believe, ye who seek honor one of another" (5:44).

Jesus now concludes the temple teaching by some pointed declarations. 1) "...he that seeth me seeth him that sent me" (12:45); 2) "I am come a light into the world" that people might walk in the light (12:46); 3) "I came not to judge the world, but to save the world" (12:47); 4) "...the

Truth—and the Blindness of Unbelief.

87

word that I have spoken, the same shall judge...in the last day" (12:48); 5) "I have not spoken of myself," but the words which the Father gave me (12:49); 6) "...his commandment is life everlasting (12:50); and 7) "...as the Father said unto me, so I speak" (12:51).

The seven great declarations give us a concise statement of the Good News of God's reconciling grace for all people of all time. The gospel is the truth of God's action to reestablish a right relationship between sinful people and Himself.

Loving Lord, Thank You for the privilege of being one of Your sheep and of being able to distinguish Your voice over the clamor of my days. AMEN.

WHAT THIS SCRIPTURE MEANS TO ME—John 10–12

Pamela and I sat on a ledge high up in the Colorado Rockies. We had tramped through the snow for a quarter of a mile and, although the temperature was below freezing, the sun was out and we were toasty warm in our parkas.

At 11,000 feet there was nothing overhead but blue sky sliced through by an occasional contrail. A stellar jay perched on a nearby rock, but when we offered him no tasty tidbit, he soon scratched us off his list and flew away. For the better part of the afternoon we sat and listened to the quiet and shared hurts and joys, disappointments and celebrations.

Pamela is my friend. She also happens to be young enough to be my daughter. For years she was the companion of one of the world's most beloved and well-known women, Corrie ten Boom. She has stayed in mansions where servants were at her beck and call, but our home is her refuge, a quiet place that she can retreat to anytime.

We laugh a lot when we're together because we know we're accepted as we are. In a world where most people mask their deepest needs and feelings, to have a friend with whom you can be honest and share authentic friendship—the kind we all need in order to be whole persons—is a treasure that many people long for and few possess.

And yet, this is the kind of relationship Jesus had with Mary and Martha and their brother Lazarus. Evidently their home in Bethany was a special haven of rest and peace for Jesus. Here were friends, loved ones, who cared for each other and shared their deepest feelings the way Pam and I do.

But in the very heart of this Scripture lesson we come upon a poignant scene. Lazarus is dead and Mary and Martha are crushed with grief. When Jesus arrives in Bethany and sees the intense pain and suffering of the two sisters, we read that He groaned in the spirit and was troubled. And then we read that "Jesus wept"—His love and concern for His grieving friends moved Him to tears.

Imagine! What a beautiful model of the kind of friendship we all want and need—Jesus, the One of whom John said earlier, "All things were made by Him; and without Him was not anything made that was made"...the One who put the rainbow in the sky...the One who said, "I am the resurrection and the life"—so loved these close friends that He felt their hurt and wept with them.

What inexplicable joy was to follow just a short time later—joy for Mary and Martha and joy for Jesus when after calling Lazarus forth from the grave, He told them to "loose him and let him go."

Then suddenly, from the resurrection of Lazarus and the celebration that must have followed, we are catapulted into the last week of Jesus' life. Once more He is with His dear friends in Bethany at a dinner being celebrated in His honor. It is at this feast that Mary annoints Jesus with costly perfume and He tells his disciples, "It is for my burial."

"What would it be like to know you had six days left to live?" I asked a young 33-year-old man that question.

He thought for a long while and then said, "I'd gather my family together and take off for the Texas Hill Country. There is a little cabin nestled in a grove of trees on the Frio River that is special to Julie and me, and I'd like to be hidden away from people. I'd want the kids to know what I consider the important things in life. I'd listen to their prayers each night, tuck them in, and sit by their beds until they dropped off to sleep. And I'd tell Julie again and again how much I love her. I'd let her know that my greatest desire for her would be that she go on living her life in the knowledge that Jesus has promised to supply all her needs."

We sat silently a few minutes longer and then he said, "Thanks for asking me that question. Little David has been begging me to teach him to fish. I've been putting him off. Tomorrow I'm going fishing with my son."

Now, in our lesson we see Jesus, just six days before His trial and death, gathering His family of disciples around Him and retreating from public life. He will perform no more miracles and won't preach any more to the multitudes. Instead, time will be spent with those He loves, teaching them truths that later the Holy Spirit will recall to their minds. He is preparing them for His death.

Corrie ten Boom told about her feelings of fear and fright when she was first introduced to the reality of death as a six-year-old child. As she poured out her feelings of fear that her daddy might die, her father very wisely told her that she had a wise Father in heaven who knew about her every need. And then he went on to explain that even when it came time to confront the reality of death, God would provide the needed strength. What a wonderful Saviour we have! Through His love for Mary and Martha and Lazarus He shows us the deep meaning and quality of friendship that we can all have through Him. And through His love for His disciples, Jesus gives them words of counsel and instruction as He prepares them for His coming death.

It is in experiences like John has given us in this lesson that we see lived out the assurance that we do indeed have a loving Father who is attentive to our every need.

LESSON 5
JOHN 13–15

Christ, the Reconciler— in Fellowship

Oh God, Use this lesson to teach me the utmost importance of having fellowship with You. AMEN.

Reconciliation with God brings us into His family. As His children through faith in Christ, we can look up and say, "Abba, Father." We belong, we fit at the throne, we have been "given the power to become the sons of God" (1:12). In Jesus we discover how children of God conduct themselves. And in belonging to God's family we must relate in love to the rest of His family.

The other Gospels tell of the Passover meal, and of the institution of the Lord's Supper. John relates the scene of footwashing...and goes on to relate the extensive teaching which Jesus gave the disciples during and at the close of the meal.

The washing of the disciples' feet is one of the most remarkable symbols of Jesus' humility and service (13:1–17). First, John tells us of Jesus' full understanding of His relationship to His coming death, to His disciples, and to His heavenly Father (13:1–3). The statement, "...that he was come from God, and went to God" supplies the contrast for the humble act of foot washing which follows. These words remind us of the great Incarnation passage in Philippians 2:5–11 where Paul affirms that Jesus was in very

Fellowship—through Loving Service.

nature God...He became in very nature man...He humbled Himself and became obedient unto death! (I suggest you stop a moment and read those seven verses.)

It was the custom in Jesus' time that as guests arrived at a house, a servant would supply water and wash their feet. But there had been no servant present on this occasion, and while John doesn't tell us, Luke described the bickering that was going on among the disciples as to which one would be the greatest in the Kingdom (Luke 22:24). This certainly hadn't produced a climate wherein any of the disciples would stoop to perform the cleansing task, so this nicety had just been bypassed and they had gone on with the supper.

Jesus, of course, was very conscious of their concern over status and took this as the occasion to model for them the role of serving. John says, "And supper being ended...he riseth from supper..." (13:2, 4a). In the Passover service there were four cups of wine that were drunk, interspersed with four promises of God. The first was with the promise, "I will bring you out." Following these words, the food was brought in and the meal was presented. Then, this question was asked, "Why is this night different from any other night?" The answer, of course, related the night to their Exodus from Egypt, and this was followed by singing the short Hallel (Ps. 113–115).

The second cup was drunk with the promise, "I will rid you of your bondage." Unleavened bread was then dipped in the dish with bitter herbs, and the head of the family prayed, "Blessed art Thou, O Lord God, King of the universe, who bringeth forth bread to eat..." The main course was then eaten—all of a roasted lamb was consumed.

The third cup was then drunk and comments were made on the expectation of the Messiah. It was at this stage in the meal that Jesus introduced "the Lord's Supper," with the symbols of His death. At the Passover meal there was normally a period of fellowship before the fourth cup was drunk. Evidently, it was at this time that Jesus got up, laid aside His outer robe, and took a towel and basin and began to wash the disciples' feet.

Later the fourth and final cup would have been shared, with the traditional words, "I will be your God and you will be my people." Then the meal closed with the singing of the last Hallel (Psa. 116–123).

Throughout the story, John shows us the "full extent" of Jesus' love, "…having loved his own which were in the world, he loved them unto the end" (13:1c). Jesus' love is seen here as He stoops to serve His disciples, as He keeps the way open for Judas to repent, as He teaches the disciples that true greatness is found in serving others (13:16; see also Luke 22:27).

As we follow Jesus in the everyday routines of our lives, we discover the greatness of serving Him in our service for others. It is the little things that enhance another person's well being; it is in the humble acts of self-giving for the enrichment of other people that we are able to express and live out the spirit of Jesus. Jesus reminded us of this eternal truth when He said, "Inasmuch as ye have done it unto one of the least of these my brethren, ye have done it unto me" (Matt. 25:40).

Fellowship is not blind; it is discerning. Our togetherness in love and acceptance is not a cover-up. We don't ignore or approve each other's limitations and shortcomings, but we refuse to allow them to disturb or impair our fellowship. Jesus was aware of the selfish ambition of Judas that led to his infamous act of betrayal. Jesus was aware of Peter's impulsive self-assertion that wasn't always backed up with inner strength—a weakness that led to Peter's denial of the Lord. And yet Jesus communicated to each one of His disciples His constant love. This truth is beautifully illustrated in this next scene in our lesson (13:18–38).

Fellowship—in the Lord's Supper.

Apparently Judas had been present when Jesus washed the disciples' feet. I can imagine that when Jesus had come to Judas that He had been especially tender, as if to say, "Judas, I haven't changed even though you have, but the way is still open for you to repent."

Now, though, Jesus announces that one of the twelve would betray Him (13:18, 21). There is no indication in this scene that any among the twelve suspected Judas of treachery. No one pointed the finger at Judas and said, "He's the one." Instead, each of them asked, "Is it I?" But Jesus knew, for God knows the innermost thoughts of our hearts.

It is likely Judas was reclining immediately to Jesus' left—close enough for them to converse without the others, hearing all that was said, for we read now that as Jesus handed Judas the sop or morsel, He sent him on his way (13:27). The others there still did not understand what was happening, but John writes that Judas left the room immediately and then adds, "It was night" (13:30). This rather sinister note has to be symbolic of the night that was in Judas' soul as he turned his back on the One who came to be the "Light of the world" and went to perform his dastardly deed.

The fact that Jesus anticipated the cross as His glorification (13:31–32) proves that for Him the redemption of the world through His coming death was His highest mission! And His words that "God shall also glorify him in himself" (13:32) express His total confidence in God and identification with Him.

In this farewell message of Jesus to His disciples He now gives them a farewell commandment, "A new commandment I give unto you, That ye love one another; as I have loved you, that ye also love one another" (13:34). On the surface it might seem rather strange that Jesus now refers to this as a *new* commandment when even in the Old Testament we are admonished to love our neighbors as ourselves (Lev. 19:18). But He does add a new dimension when He says "as I have loved you." Jesus' love, opening Himself to us, is to the extent of death.

If we love others as He loves us, we will open ourselves to others to meet their needs whatever the cost to us! This then becomes the proof of our discipleship—our expression of love reflects His love. And by this love—not by our words, our doctrine, our traditions—the world will recognize that we know Jesus.

A vivid illustration of love's cost is seen in the story of Mary C. Funk, a young Mennonite woman, who was returning many years ago to America on furlough from mission work in India. She first sailed from India to England and then boarded the Titanic for America. When the ship struck an iceberg and was sinking, Mary Funk was soon safely aboard a lifeboat. But then as she looked out across the deck, she saw a young woman clutching a child to her breast. Since the lifeboat was filled, Mary Funk got out and gave her place to the woman and child.

From our studies in all of the Gospels we've learned that Jesus' method of teaching in parables was very effective, and sometimes rather than tell a story He gave a parabolic statement. That is what He did here when, in response to Peter's question, "Lord, wither goest thou? Jesus answered him, whither I go, thou canst not follow me now..." (13:36). Then Peter's question for clarity led to his assertion that he was willing to die for Jesus. There can be no doubt about Peter's sincerity at the moment, but Jesus knew of his weakness and said, "The cock shall not crow, till thou hast denied me thrice" (13:38). And while John doesn't mention it here, we are reminded that in Luke Jesus told Peter that "Satan hath desired to have you...But I have prayed for thee, that thy faith shall fail not" (Luke 22:31–32).

In spite of the fact that we, like Peter, don't fully understand ourselves and our faith is often shaky, we can take courage in the truth that Jesus doesn't give up on us any more than He did with Peter.

What is God like? This is the question that has intrigued many great minds throughout human history. And it is answered simply in the verses we turn our attention to now (14:1–14)—God is like Jesus, "...he that hath seen me hath seen the Father" (14:9).

Fellowship—in Jesus as the Way.

My friend, William Schubert, who was a Methodist missionary in the Orient for fifty years, has told this unusual story. It seems that Mao Tse Tung was seen scribbling on a piece of paper during a particularly boring committee session. After a time he crumpled up the paper and tossed it into the wastebasket, once again entering into the conversation. After the meeting was over a reporter picked the paper from the basket and read these words, "Is there a God? And if so, how can I, an old man, find him?"

We don't know for certain whether that story is truth or fiction, but there's one thing we know for sure—the answer is in Jesus Christ! He *is* the Good News of the gospel. In our lesson now He proclaims boldly, "I am the way, the truth, and the life: no man cometh unto the Father, but by me" (14:6).

At the very beginning of this part of our Scripture lesson Jesus seeks to calm the hearts and minds of His disciples— they believe in God, now they are to believe in the Son who has open access to the Father and to the Father's house (14:1–3). Jesus assured His disciples then and us now that while He must be away for a time, He will come again (14:3) and escort us into our heavenly home. We don't know when He will return. It could be tomorrow, or not for another thousand years. It will happen when His plans and purposes are fulfilled.

From our house on a ridge at Harrisonburg, Virginia, I can look out across the Shenandoah Valley to the mountain range beyond. Between me and the top of those distant mountains there are many hills and valleys which I'm unable to see. That is how it is as we attempt to view the great future event of Christ's return—there are many years of experience between the cross and His second coming, but He fixes our attention to the high point!

Jesus concludes the discussion about seeing the Father and responds to Philip's question with the amazing claim, "I am in the Father, and the Father in me" (14:11). And the validity of this claim is found in both Jesus' words and His actions. The lesson for us here is that as children of God—Christians in the twentieth-century world—when we open our lives completely to God, His will can be done in and through us as we strive with Christ's help to do those things that please the Father.

Finally, we find in verses 13 and 14 a remarkable promise for us in prayer. But it is conditioned by two phrases: "That the Father may be glorified in the Son," and "Ask anything in my name." Asking for our own glory violates the condition. Similarly, asking over our own name or claim rather than asking according to the name of Jesus invalidates His promise. He promises to answer, but in the same context in which He affirmed the oneness between Himself and the Father, a oneness, a unity, into which we are to participate. Unity is a sense of oneness in the fellowship of Christ. At the World Congress on Evangelism in Berlin, 1966, there was a great sense of this fellowship across national and denominational lines. When George Beverly Shea got up to sing, he said, "If my old dad was here, he would say, 'Son, the wheat is so tall that we can't even see the fences.'"

Now, to understand fully what Jesus is saying in verses 13 and 14 we need to look again to verse 12—a promise that has often been misinterpreted, "...greater works than these shall he do; because I go unto my Father" (14:12). It is the completion of Jesus' redemptive mission and His return to the Father that assures us of answers to prayer. It is the finished work of Christ that gives us full access to God! Believing in Jesus opens the way for us to participate in His work—the ongoing and redeeming good news of salvation through Jesus Christ that crosses all class, racial, cultural, and national lines and builds up the "body of Christ" across the world through the transforming work of the Holy Spirit.

Someone has interpreted fellowship as "two fellows in the same ship!" Fellowship does mean togetherness, a sense of belonging that is expressed in loving openness with one another. And now Jesus continues His teaching in this part of our lesson (14:15–31) by saying, "If ye love me"—keep your life open to Me—"Keep my commandments." The true measure of our love for God is found in our obedience to Him and His will for our lives. Or, to put it another way, a continuous love for God is our best safeguard against disobedience.

Fellowship—in the Presence of the Spirit.

The full meaning of this "safeguard" is expressed as the presence of the Holy Spirit. Consequently, Jesus now says that He will ask the Father to give us *another* Comforter, the Holy Spirit, "that he may abide with you forever" (14:16). The Greek word translated, "Comforter" is *parakletos* and it refers to "another of like kind"—the Holy Spirit is like Jesus. He will help us handle all circumstances of life. As we reflect on Jesus' words here, we see that He is our Advocate (legal assistant) with the Father, and the Holy Spirit is the Father's Advocate with us as believers in Jesus. The Father's Advocate is the "Spirit of truth" (14:7) who will keep us from error, guide us into all truth, and give us spiritual insight which the world lacks (read 1 Cor. 2:1–13).

In this marvelous passage that has brought reassurance and confidence to Christians of all time, Jesus speaks of the Father, the Son, the Holy Spirit, the disciples, the world, and the prince of this world (Satan) as He rolls back the curtain on the deepest meanings of reconciliation. Jesus and the Father express the deepest "togetherness"—"I am in my father" (14:20). Jesus and the disciples experience "togetherness"—"I will not leave you...I will come to you" (14:18, 19, 21, 23). The Holy Spirit and the disciples experience intimate "togetherness"—"...he dwelleth with you and shall be in you...he shall teach you all things" (14:16–17, 26). By implication, the body of Christ—

the church—experiences a "togetherness" that the world does not know (14:21–24). And this fellowship transcends the power or influence of the "ruler of the world," the devil, for he has no power over Christ. In fact, the clash with the "ruler of the world" which came at the Cross showed people of all time how authentically Jesus lived by the will of the Father. Christ's victory in love, even to death, would "unmask" principalities and powers so that we would have a choice between the way of the world and the life of Christ (see Col. 2:15).

This emphasis on "togetherness" is now followed by Jesus' great gift of peace, "Peace I leave with you, my peace I give unto you: not as the world giveth, give I unto you. Let not your heart be troubled, neither let it be afraid" (14:27). Peace—*Shalom* is the traditional Jewish greeting that implies not just absence of conflict but total well-being. Jesus' peace is His gracious identification with us, the full well-being of our "togetherness," our fellowship with the Father. He then goes on to emphasize that fellowship by a reference to His going to the Father who is "greater than I" (14:28). In other words Jesus is saying that our Father—God—is indeed everything we have seen in the Son but, that there is much more to God than the Incarnate Son has been free to express in the limitations of His humanness (see Phil. 2:5–11).

These particular words of Jesus are a part of His last teaching before His death. This makes them especially meaningful to us. Some twenty years ago I was listening to the news and heard that at the University of Oklahoma one of the professors, Dr. Buchanan, had given a short lecture the evening before as a part of what had been billed as "The Last Lecture Series." Dr. Buchanan's assignment had been to address the audience as if the words spoken would be his last. These fifteen words comprised his entire lecture: "Every day help somebody, every day exercise mind and body, every day contact your God."

In this part of Jesus' last teaching before the Cross it is important for us to note the emphasis on love and obedience. These two words are not contradictory; they are really complementary. When love is understood as opening ones' life intimately to another, then love for God is obedience. When obedience is understood as an attitude before it is an act, then obedience to God is love. And when both are seen together in reconciliation, as relational, there is freedom from legalism of all kinds.

The practical good news from these words of Jesus is that He calls us into togetherness, into family; we belong. He calls us into "togetherness," into the family of God—*we belong*.

Jesus now gives us the parable of the vine (15:1–8). This parable of the believer's relation to Christ is personal, but it is also universal, for it employs a trans-cultural figure. In many countries the vine is known as the source of food and drink; it is a remarkable figure of communication. Jesus may have selected the symbol from the "Lord's Supper" which He had just instituted. Or He may have selected it because the vine was a symbol of Israel (Psa. 80) and was carved over the temple gate.

Fellowship—by Abiding in Christ.

Jesus' listeners and John's early readers would have remembered Isaiah's description of Israel and Judah as the vineyard and vine of God (5:1–7). Here we see the vineyard is a disappointment to God. Jeremiah added that the noble vine had turned into a degenerate plant (2:21). And Hosea described Israel as an "empty vine, he bringeth forth fruit unto himself" (10:1).

It is against this background that Jesus asserts boldly, "I am the true vine" (15:1). Then He adds immediately that "my Father is the husbandman," and in verse 5 the picture is completed as Jesus says, "...ye are the branches."

In pursuing my hobby of cultivating vines and trees I have learned how important it is to trim the branches, for when they are left untrimmed, they have less vitality and some die. And when a vine or tree is not pruned, the fruit is of a much poorer quality, and sometimes there may not be any fruit at all. There is far greater risk in underpruning than overpruning.

In this parable Jesus now compares the Father to the husbandman—the one who cares for the vines and prunes them as needed. The point is that anything that stands in the way of our living fruitful lives must be removed even though it might be painful. This reminds us of the words, "...whom the Lord loveth he chasteneth..." (Heb. 12:6).

Jesus next tells us that when we live fruitful and productive lives, we honor and give glory to the Father (15:8), and, of course, it is this that is the real evidence that we are truly Jesus' disciples. Significantly, as we turn to Galatians and read about the "fruit of the Spirit" (5:22), it is clear that this "fruit" is not expressed or practiced in private, but is seen in our relationship with others. Ours is not a faith of isolation but must be expressed in our day-to-day lives with family and "neighbors" near and far.

But the key to bearing fruit for God—for living productive and fruitful Christian lives—is possible only as we abide in Him. It is Christ's life in us that bears the fruit. Just as the sap of the vine flows into the branches to give life to produce fruit, so it is the energy of Christ, the life of Christ, in us that produces fruitful lives.

Jesus also makes it clear that the promise of answered prayer (15:7) is conditioned by our abiding in Him as He gives us one of the great promises found in the Gospels, "If ye abide in me, and my words abide in you, ye shall ask what ye will, and it shall be done unto you." In other words, the branch that abides in the vine, and participates in the vine-life—the Word of God—can then ask anything that extends the purpose of the vine and it shall be done!

Fellowship—in the Practice of Love.

Our relationship with God is one of love more than of the law. Contrary to the impression of many Christians, the law was under love even in the Old Testament, for in the Ark of the Covenant (Ex. 25:10–22) the tables of the law were kept *under* the Mercy Seat. Salvation has always been by God's mercy, by God's forgiving grace, not by adherance to the law. And yet one who lives in God's love lives in devotion to His will or His law. Psalm 119 is a remarkable testimony to this, for in all but two of its one hundred and seventy-six verses there is a loving reference to the laws of God.

Jesus has opened for us a new understanding of this love-level of relationship with God, and now in this part of our lesson (15:9–17) He builds on this truth, "As the Father hath loved me"—totally, unreservedly, in full identification with Him—"so have I loved you"—totally, unreservedly in full identification with us. And, having said that, Jesus commands us to "continue ye in my love"—a call for us to maintain a total, full identification with Him at all times. Jesus then adds that to keep His commandments, to do His will, is to abide in His love (15:10).

In this marvelous lesson on the love theme we learn that the fellowship of love is:

- the way to joy, the joy of belonging;
- response-love, the experience initiated by Jesus;
- self-giving, even to the extent of death (15:13);
- friendship at the deepest level of loyalty.

Life in Christ—the Good News of the gospel—is an expression of the commandment to love: first, to love God with our whole selves, and second, to love others as we love ourselves. And this great commandment is underlined here as Jesus says, "...love one another, as I have loved you" (15:12)—totally, unreservedly, even to the point of dying for us. Jesus then builds on this great love theme by elevating the position of His disciples and us to that of friends, "Ye are my friends, if ye do whatever I command you. Henceforth I call you not servants...but I have called you friends" (15:14–15). We are His friends as we live in His love. And this friendship makes us full partners in His mission. What a marvelous truth! You and I are in partnership with Jesus Christ!

The initiative of divine grace is expressed in Jesus' words when He says, "Ye have not chosen me, but I have chosen you..." (15:16). At the time, these words, of course, had primary meaning for the twelve disciples, but their greater meaning includes you and me. Our faith does not originate with a blind search for God, but is our response to God who has chosen us to live fruitful—fruit-bearing—lives and at the same time has given us assurance that whatever we ask in His name, in His purpose, the Father will give us. This is His promise to us as members of the family of God.

Again, in verse 17 Jesus repeats the commandment to "love one another." This is the third time He has stressed this theme in these verses, for the heart of the ethic of discipleship is love. John was so impressed with Jesus' emphasis on the importance of love that in writing his first epistle he expanded at length on it in the third and fourth chapters. Here, with apparent reference to Jesus' own words in our Gospel lesson John writes, "And this is his commandment, That we should believe on the name of his Son Jesus Christ, and love one another, as he gave us commandment...And this commandment have we from him, That he who loveth God love his brother also" (1 John 3:23; 4:21).

In the late 1960s a church in Portland, Oregon, had a group that set out to evangelize and invite hippies to church. One Sunday morning a young man with long, stringy hair and dressed in the offbeat hippy garb of those years walked into the church and moved down the aisle looking for a seat. No one moved to make room for him to be seated, so he continued to the front, and then sat down cross-legged in the aisle.

A chill seemed to move across that congregation. Suddenly, an older deacon, carrying a cane, got up from where he was sitting and made his way down the aisle. When he came to where the young man was sitting, he laid down his cane and sat down cross-legged beside him. The pastor, standing quietly at the podium, broke the silence as he said with choked voice, "What I say this morning you will not long remember, but what you have just seen you will never forget!"

Fellowship—in Separation from the World.

In these closing verses of our lesson (15:18–27) Jesus drives home the point that while His disciples in all time are in the world, we are not "of the world" (15:19). Our citizenship is in heaven (Phil. 3:20). We are, first of all, members of the Kingdom of God. And contrary to what seems to happen so often, we are to build up and encourage our brothers and sisters in Christ even though at times their understanding of "what Jesus would do" in a given situation may differ from ours. This is what is involved in loving one another.

At the same time Jesus warns the disciples that the world will reject and hate them even as it does Him. The Christian's identification with Christ is an affront to the world. The same spirit that rejects Jesus rejects those who identify with Him.

In the first centuries of the church, in the Roman Empire, every citizen was expected to offer a "pinch of incense" and say, "Caesar is Lord." Then when that little ritual was out of the way, they could serve any god they chose at a secondary level to Caesar. But the Christians refused to do this, and they were hated and hounded and even martyred for saying simply, "Jesus is Lord!" They refused to in any way compromise in their commitment to Christ even though the cost of their separation was high.

But our separation as Christians is not first and foremost from the world, it is *to* Christ. By being committed to Jesus we will be selective about all other commitments. "The servant is not greater than his lord" (15:20), consequently, as we are faithful to God in our witness, we can expect rejection and opposition. Kierkegaard reminds us that "danger faces Christians whenever they cease to be in tension with the popular mentality." And that danger is equally present today even though it may take different forms. For some, it is not being accepted by the "in group." For others, the danger may be in the form of emotional and psychological repression. Then there are those even today who face prison and bodily harm because they refuse to offer their "pinch of incense."

The presence of Christ exposed the sin of the world (15:22), and this is most clearly revealed at Calvary. At the cross the world said in effect, "We'd rather get rid of God than serve Him," for to reject Jesus was, and is, to reject God.

We have seen in this lesson that our role as Christians is to be in fellowship first with God through Jesus Christ and then with one another. We are to love as we are loved, and we are to be witnesses in society of the family of God. And it is our witness to Christ that brings about our separation from the world. Jesus foresaw all of this, and, now in verse 26 He promises the Comforter, the Holy Spirit who is given to enable and secure our witness. As members of the family of God, we are called to be the light of the world, punching holes in the darkness.

Thank You for the ministry of the Comforter in my life. He guides me when I need direction; comforts me when I grieve; and encourages me to live for You! AMEN.

WHAT THIS SCRIPTURE MEANS TO ME—John 13–15

In this lesson Jesus was eating the last meal that He would share with His disciples before His death. They were all there in that upper room reclining around the table in the style of the times. John was reclining on Jesus' right side, and according to tradition Judas Iscariot was reclining on Jesus' left, the place of honor. Only after the events of the night would the disciples recognize that the one they had trusted to be their treasurer was a traitor.

During the course of the meal Jesus got up from the table, laid aside His outer clothes, and gave the disciples and us a vivid object lesson on the important truth about what it means to be a servant in our relationships with other people. He washed and cleansed the feet of every man in the room, *even Judas*. In this act we catch a glimpse of the gentle, caring, and humble spirit that characterized Jesus' words and actions. And He gave us the supreme model for our day-to-day attitudes and actions.

Only when Jesus had dismissed Judas with "be quick about your business" and he had gone out into the night to betray his Lord did Jesus begin the great teachings that He wanted to burn into the hearts of these men who were to be entrusted with the good news of the gospel. Among these final words of Jesus was the new commandment, the one that transcends all others—love one another.

Tradition tells us that when the Apostle John was an old man his students flocked around him and asked for one last word on living the Christian life. He replied with the words of Jesus, "Little children love one another." Although they repeatedly asked him to add more to that, he refused. Upon being pressed further he finally said, "Little children love one another" and then he added, "All else is anathema."

How refreshing and wonderful it is in a world torn apart by so much hate and bitterness and inhumanity to read that the *agape* love of Jesus Christ is still being practiced by people whose names may never make the headlines of the newspaper. But in their quiet way they are living out the new commandment that Jesus gave to His disciples (and to all of us) that night at the Last Supper.

Recently, I was deeply moved to read about a young man from Colombia, South America, who had come to the United States to attend college. It came out that some of his friends were members of the terrorist group that in March of 1981 had murdered Chester Bitterman III, a young linguist with Wycliffe Bible Translators' Summer Institute of Linguistics.

This young man admitted that his friends were puzzled by two things. First, they had been sure that Wycliffe would agree to abandon their work in Colombia in exchange for the young missionary's life—which they refused to do. And next, the terrorists were unable to understand how Chester Bitterman's parents could donate an ambulance to the people of Colombia in memory of their son. The young man's friends had expected bitterness and hatred and revenge, not this act of love. In fact, Mrs. Bitterman, Chester's mother, is reported to have said, "We're able to do this because God has taken the hatred out of our hearts."

Jesus' commandment to love one another is not an option. Rather, it is the stigmata on the followers of Jesus. This is the kind of love that the Bittermans had for the people of Colombia; it is the kind of love that Mother Teresa has for the sick and the dying on the streets of Calcutta; and it is the kind of love that Charles Colson and Prison Fellowship members have for the thousands of people in prison all across the United States.

This new commandment became the identifying characteristic of the early Christians. Many things have changed since the first century when Jesus spoke these words, but living out this same spirit of love on a day-to-day basis is still the chief characteristic of Christians today.

LESSON 6
JOHN 16–17

Christ the Reconciler—in Unity

Master, Help me to learn this lesson and to pass on to others what I learn. AMEN.

The family of God is a new community reconciled in Christ. With a diversity of culture, race, class, personality, etc., we are united in one body as the people of God. The twelve disciples are an example of this oneness, this quality of unity. No one but Jesus could enable Simon the Zealot and Matthew the tax collector to walk as brothers! No one but Jesus could unite James and John, the sons of thunder, and Andrew, the caring enabler. Jesus is creating a new people that are united around Him.

Unity—through the Work of the Spirit.

Knowing as He did what lay ahead for His disciples in the way of testing and persecution, Jesus now speaks to the importance of their unity in the Spirit (16:1–16). It is through the work of God's Spirit in our lives that we have the boldness to confront possible persecution and even death, and not only confront that fear, but overcome it. For as with the Spirit's help we overcome our fear of death, we will at the same time overcome our fear of life. This is important in our daily walk as Christians, for if we live under the fear of failure and death, we are unable to assume the risks of living boldly for God.

The disciples are warned here that they may be isolated and put out of the synagogues—banned from their customary places of worship—but their unity with God through the Holy Spirit will take them through their times of trial. Jesus spoke to the fear of persecution and death by setting it in the larger context of the Kingdom of the Father in conflict with the kingdoms of this world. And He could speak of going to the Father with such joy that leaving this world was relegated to its proper place—accepted but not courted (16:1–6).

The ultimate meaning of the Kingdom of God is the presence and rule of God among us. Jesus, anticipating His coming departure (16:5), now gives some very significant and pointed teaching about the coming of the Holy Spirit, God's other Presence. In saying, "It is expedient for you that I go away" (16:7), we come to understand Christ's awareness that while His presence localizes God in Jesus of Nazareth, His physical departure from this earth would permit God's universal presence in the person of the Holy Spirit. Earlier Jesus had said that He would ask the Father and He would send the Spirit to the disciples. But now Jesus says, "I will send him unto you." It is this combined word that is expressed so clearly in the creed of Nicea, A.D. 325, that the Spirit proceeds from the Father *and* the Son.

The Spirit's presence is God's presence, extending His rule in the world through those who are open to Him. Thirty years ago, I was a young pastor in Sarasota, Florida, and it was my privilege to introduce Dr. William Culbertson, who at that time was president of Moody Bible Institute, to my congregation. On that occasion Dr. Culbertson preached from this sixteenth chapter of John, and he highlighted the three things Jesus said the Spirit would do in the following way: 1) He will convince the world of sin because they believe not, by showing the world faith through *our* believing; 2) He will convince the world of righteousness after Jesus has returned to the Father by the witness of *our* righteous lives; 3) He will convince the world of judgment by showing that Satan is judged and defeated now in our lives as we witness to freedom.

I heard one time about a family vacation cabin in New England that was known for the good cold water that for many years had come from the open well in the front yard. Years later, a member of the family who had enjoyed the cabin as a boy, now took his own family to New England for a vacation at the old, familiar place. When they hurried to the front yard to draw fresh water, they found that the well was dry! In consternation they asked the local plumber what had happened and were told that in drilling another well to supply the indoor plumbing, they had stopped using the old well. As a result of disuse, silt had built up and the well had finally gone dry. This is a parable of sorts of the importance of our actively walking in the Spirit every day of our lives—otherwise we become careless and face the danger of going dry.

We come to understand here that the Spirit is God's supervisory agent in the ongoing life and direction of the church. He enriches the church by 1) guiding us into all truth; 2) glorifying Christ in us; and 3) taking of the grace of Christ and sharing it with us. The reference that "...he shall not speak of himself" (16:13b) should be translated, "He will not speak from Himself." In other words, He will not speak independently from the Father and the Son, but He will impart and illuminate the revelation of the Father in the Son.

Jesus now assures the disciples that although He will be leaving them physically, they will see Him again (16:16). And this remains our hope as we look and work expectantly for His second coming.

Jesus' teaching here on unity in the Spirit carries important overtones for us today. It is essential that we not become so preoccupied with our understanding or form or interpretation of the faith that we become belligerent and critical of our brothers and sisters in Christ. Rather, we should devote our time and energies to an understanding and a world view of God's Word. For the Holy Spirit inspired the Word, and He will illuminate our minds to understand it. This is the same Spirit that calls us to Christ, and as we are open to Him, He will transform us into the likeness of Christ.

Unity—in the Spirit of Joy.

In response to the questions that raged in the disciples' minds, Jesus now turns His attention to that quality of joy which is the believer's birthright, which transcends any temporary separation or time of sorrow (16:17–24). He wants His disciples and us to see that joy is a relational experience. It is a "high" of belonging, of fellowship. Joy is wholistic, for it is a matter of spirit and affects the whole of life. It has dimensions of anticipation, of participation, and of fulfillment. The writer of the Epistle to the Hebrews says of Jesus, "...who for the joy that was set before him endured the cross, despising the shame, and is set down at the right hand of the throne of God" (Heb, 12:2).

Joy is an atmosphere of acceptance, of good-will, of being participants in something of "meaning." By its very spirit, joy unifies; it binds us together at the spiritual level of life. As Christians, we are united in worship and praise. We find this expressed a little later in the Gospel as Jesus shares His joy in His oneness with the Father and in turn invites us into oneness with Him (17:20–23). And as we experience that oneness—that unity with God the Father and with Jesus—the joy of the Lord dominates all of life.

But this experience of transitional thinking was not easy for the disciples. They were too close to the woods to see the trees. Because they were still expecting His Kingdom to be a socio-political rule that would subdue their enemies, they did not yet see the Kingdom of God as a Messianic order that is primarily spiritual and ethical. This was an ongoing struggle for the disciples, and because of it they were often uncertain about Jesus. Jesus knew there could be no joy in uncertainty. Joy is interfaced with assurance. And so by His words and actions He provided this assurance.

Hundreds of years before, Nehemiah had captured the power and attractiveness of joy when he said "…the joy of the Lord is your strength" (Neh. 8:10). It is with the spirit of joy that we achieve strength" and unity and become appealing and winsome witnesses of the gospel of Christ. Sam Shoemaker, a powerful Christian voice of a generation or two ago, said one time that "Joy, I suspect, is the most attractive quality in the world."

We see also in our study that Jesus' words of assurance (16:19–24) to His disciples are given in the context of His anticipation of His coming death. His comment about their grief that would turn to joy implies His full awareness of the cross and the resurrection.

Then in verse 21 when He likened His death and resurrection to travail and birth, He was looking ahead to the beginning of the new age, a time of full reconciliation with the Father. While the disciples did not fully understand what Jesus meant by all of this, there is no doubt that the full meaning of His promises came to them after the cross and empty tomb were realities. In a similar way, the meanings of many biblical passages become clear to us only after we have personally entered into their meaning. It is then that the spirit of rejoicing enriches our lives, and His special joy becomes the witness and radiance of the gospel.

The privilege of full reconciliation is ours in Christ. We can look up and say, "Abba, Father; I'm one of your children, and I have access to the throne!" And in that confidence we have the promise that the Father will give us whatever we ask in Jesus' name "...Whatsoever ye shall ask the Father in my name, he will give it you. Hitherto ye have asked nothing in my name: ask and ye shall receive, that your joy may be full" (16:23–24). There is no partial measure promised here. Our joy is complete because through Jesus Christ we're able to have audience with God the Father Himself.

Unity—in a Community of Faith.

Each community of people has a primary focus. For some it is class, for others it is economic interests or political commitments, ethnic values, or racial or cultural identity. But for the disciples of Jesus Christ, our focus is a faith relationship with God the Father. Even so, within the Christian church we are often divided by the same diversity of focus that fragments the world. And yet we know there is no Christian culture as such. No one group or denomination has captured the Kingdom! And no nationalism has an edge on the grace of God.

But as we turn our attention to Jesus' words now (16:25–33), three things stand out, 1) we are in God's love when we are in Jesus' love (16:27); 2) we need to understand Jesus if we are to have an intelligent faith (16:29–30); and, 3) Jesus has overcome the world and enabled us to have "peace" and "good cheer," (16:32–33).

Jesus came from the Father and entered the world, and having made that major adjustment, He now viewed His death and resurrection as the next adjustment to return to the Father. And the great affirmation that comes to us is that just as Jesus faced death in full confidence that the Father would raise Him up, so we face death in full confidence in Jesus' promise to raise us up!

The community of Jesus is a community of faith. In writing to the Ephesian Christians Paul asserted that there is "One Lord, one faith, one baptism, One God and Father of all, who is above all, and through all, and in you all" (Eph. 4:5). We are initiated by Jesus into *one* community of faith. Jesus entered the world to create this special people. Cannon Michael Green said at the Lausanne Congress on

Evangelism, "We must discover that the church itself is part of the gospel." The mission of the church—the community of faith is to offer the broken and lonely people in today's world a *new community* in Christ. And He reconciles us to Himself to be this people, promising that "in me ye might have peace" (16:33). And He assures us of victory as His people, for even in the face of impending death Jesus says, "I have overcome the world."

In a few days the powers of evil in the world killed His body, but they did not crush His spirit, for on the third day He was victorious over death. And even as the world could not defeat Jesus, it cannot defeat us—our victory is a matter of spirit as His was. It is seen in our joy and peace, which are not dependent upon what happens *to* us but *within* us. This peace resides in us and produces an inner harmony that radiates our joy and witnesses to our community with God. Jesus *is* our peace. And faith unites us to Him and permits Him to be Himself *in us*!

Unity—in Personal Prayer.

There is nothing that expresses the true spirit of one's life as does prayer. When we address God it becomes clear just how well we know Him, how honest we are with Him, and how we seek to relate to Him. Self-interests show up immediately in our prayers. Reverence, or lack of it, is evident in our prayers. In fact, prayer reveals who is actually in charge of our lives—frequently it seems that the one praying is really "in charge" and is merely attempting to use God as a cosmic bellhop.

But true prayer is communion with God; it is not talking God into doing something. And it is certainly not overcoming God's reluctance or an attempt to "twist God's arm." Rather, prayer is laying hold of God's willingness. It is conditioning ourselves to God's will so that He has the moral freedom to carry out what He has been wanting to do for some time but for which He had to await our participation.

Jesus' prayer in the seventeenth chapter of John is the ultimate example of true reverence and communion with God. First, in the opening verses (17:1–5) we discover that the personal base of prayer is in the privilege of addressing God as "Father," for the purpose in prayer is that He should be glorified (17:1). And the priorities of personal prayer are established so that we can fulfill the work God has asked us to do (17:4). This is the highest priority for every day of our lives—to "finish the work" God has given us to do for that day.

Then, too, we learn that prayer follows the "laws" of Divine grace. There are laws of gravity, laws of seasons (we don't plant corn in December), and laws of relationship. These laws of prayer must not be broken, for prayer does not misuse God, rather it conforms us to the will of God.

Prayer is also the clearest expression of the character of our theology. We tend to complicate things so much with lengthy and involved explanations and arguments about biblical and doctrinal aspects of our understanding of God. But I think we would do well to heed the attitude of Dr. Karl Barth, the famous Swiss theologian. When he was asked to share the greatest thought that ever crossed his mind, he answered after a brief pause. "Jesus loves me, this I know, for the Bible tells me so."

In the opening lines of Jesus' prayer we are given in simple and understandable form the interpretation of eternal life, "And this is life eternal, that they might know thee, the only true God, and Jesus Christ whom thou hast sent" (17:3). And building on this interpretation the Westminster Confession states that our primary purpose as Christians is "to glorify God and to *enjoy Him forever.*"

We also find in these opening personal words, "And now, O Father, glorify thou me with thine own self with the glory which I had with thee before the world was" (17:5) that Jesus was looking ahead to the agony of the cross. The extent of Jesus' commitment to our salvation is expressed here as He sees the cross as the expression of the glory of God's grace. And we see Jesus' great integrity of purpose as He uses the authority God had given Him to serve us, to give us eternal life, here and forever. But not only did Jesus pray for His disciples and us then—He continues to pray for us now. Paul underlined this truth when he wrote, "It is Christ that died, yea rather, that is risen again, who is even at the right hand of God, who also maketh intercession for us" (Rom. 8:34).

Unity—in Prayer for Disciples.

"Hear, O Israel: the Lord our God is one..." These words from Deuteronomy 6:4 are known as the *Shema* and are at the heart of the Judaic-Christian understanding of God. And by "one" we mean "oneness"—not a mathematical or numerical "one." But with all of the Old Testament declarations about God, He is known adequately only in Jesus (John 14:9). And now as Jesus prays for His disciples (17:6–12), He says, "I have manifested thy name unto the men which thou gavest me…" (17:6).

At the same time Jesus expresses the nature of Divine initiative in calling out "a people of God." It is God who moves *to* us in grace. The initiative is with Him. This is the unique difference between Christianity and the other religions of the world. While the others are involved in a search to find God, salvation by grace through Jesus Christ means that God has taken the initiative and come to us. So Jesus in this prayer sees His disciples, and us, as a gift of God to Him. Paul elaborated on this truth when he wrote the Ephesian Christians and explained that we are Christ's inheritance (Eph. 1:18). We are His people; we belong to Him (17:7–8).

This is a marvelous truth which you and I need to claim every day of our lives. Our late twentieth-century world is extremely complex both in relationships and technology. It seems that we live under an oppressive cloud of violence and threat of war. The insidious increase of drug use and teenage suicide compounds our feelings of inability to cope. But even with all of this we are told in this prayer of Jesus that we are His! And as members of His fellowship of believers, we are assured that in His power we can handle anything that comes our way.

In verse 9 Jesus makes it clear that He is praying for His disciples and not for the world. His prayer now is for the men and women who follow Him—who go out to win the world in Jesus' name. Then He makes a statement that would be audacious if He were not the Son of God, "And all mine are thine, and thine are mine" (17:10). Next He asks the Father to keep the disciples "through thine own name"—"Holy Father…everlasting Father," the name given to the Christ, (Isa. 9:6). And finally, He prays that His disciples "may be one" as the Father and Son are one (17:11).

We must ask the question: in what ways was Jesus saying that He and the Father are one? What is the character of this oneness to which we are called? What is the meaning of "that name" which the Father gave to Jesus and by which He kept the twelve disciples except for Judas who chose to live contrary to the Name? Perhaps the key is in the last name in the list in Isaiah 9:6, "the Prince of Peace." This is the name that binds us together as one. Jesus and the Father can be seen as one in: *purpose*, "I have finished the work which thou gavest me to do" (17:4); in *mutual honor*, "...glorify thy Son, that thy Son also may glorify thee" (17:1); and in full *partnership*, "And all mine are thine, and thine are mine" (17:10). And the oneness to which Jesus calls us is to be of the same character—it is not a surface unity but a deep sense of togetherness in the reconciling grace of God.

Prayer makes us partners—we are participants in God's work. In parts of the west and southwest I have seen great pipelines that are laid to carry oil from the oil fields to refineries many miles away. But in order for these pipelines to function there are pumping stations every thirty miles that push the oil along to its ultimate destination. As partners in God's work in our world, our task is similar in a way to those pumping stations, for as we share with one another, we are carrying the good work of God's love and grace along.

Unity—in Prayer for Sanctity.

Holiness means that we belong completely to God, that we are wholly His. The consequence or subjective aspect of holiness or sanctification is wholeness, the correcting of our perversions and the healing of our broken selves. And this brokenness or self-centeredness is the basic obstacle to oneness. Hence Jesus' prayer for oneness moves to the plea for His disciples to be sanctified by the Truth (17:13–19).

Jesus begins by telling us that it is through a wholistic relationship with the Father that we experience the full joy of Christ (17:13). This is the joy of belonging, of assurance, of being God's own possession. As such, we are not of the world, but members of the family of God. Twice in these verses Jesus says that His disciples are not of the world, just as He is not of the world (17:14, 16). At the same time, though, we understand that Jesus did not pray for His disciples to be taken out of the world (17:15). Christianity is not an escape or other-wordly religion. Instead, we have the promise of victory through Christ in the ordinary and everyday affairs of life.

Perhaps our best example is that of Jesus who was *in* the world but not *of* it—He was with people, healing, helping, encouraging. We, too, are called as He was to be agents of reconciliation, to be healers—ambassadors of Christ (2 Cor. 5:19–20). We are extensions of the presence of

Christ, witnesses for Him in our world today. And witnessing is done by presence, service, and communication—in that order.

In verse 17 we find a very important petition in Jesus' prayer, "Sanctify them through thy truth: thy word is truth" (17:17). The Truth of God is expressed in the Word of God—the Word made flesh, that is Jesus, and the Word taught and written. In the written Word that is inspired by the Spirit we meet the Christ, the Word personified. And in Jesus we are meeting God—He is the Word, the revealer of God (17:2). It is this truth that calls us, that sets us apart as God's people, that sanctifies or makes us holy.

This part of our lesson closes now as Jesus identifies with His disciples when He says, "And for their sakes I sanctify myself, that they also might be sanctified through the truth" (17:19). In other words, Jesus sets Himself apart from the world of self-interest to be totally God's person. And in so doing Jesus opens the way through the cross for us to become fully and totally God's persons. We are set apart in unity with Him to live whole and productive lives.

Unity—in Prayer for All who Believe.

Futuristic prayer is one's belief in the ongoing work of God. He is the main actor on the stage of history, carrying out His work. We pray believing that He continues to work. In our time, despite world hunger, violence, and the nuclear threat, we can still pray believing that God's providential care assures a future for this world.

Jesus prayed not only for those with whom He had shared His life but for all who would come to believe in Him down through the thousands of years (17:20–26). He prayed for you and me. He prayed that we might be one with Him and the Father. Notice the expression "...that they also may be one *in us*" (17:21, italics mine). We also are to be one, along with the disciples who composed His immediate group. This oneness is a unity of persons and purpose in the midst of our diversity.

The heart of Jesus' prayer for all future believers is the prayer for oneness (17:21-23). The body of Christ is one, and the diversity of its parts is not a division in the body. With all of our cultural and philosophical conditioning which separates us into so many denominations we must avoid idolizing any theological group and see ourselves as a part of the church universal, the one body of Christ.

The unity for which Jesus prayed is not structurally or

institutionally negotiated. Rather it is a reconciliation of Spirit, a being made mature in oneness (17:23). And this oneness, which transcends our self-centeredness, becomes a primary witness to the world of the reconciling grace of God (17:21, 23).

In our congregation in Washington, D.C. we have looked for new ways to witness to this unity. While we are affiliated with the Mennonite Church, we are inter-denominational as a congregation. We have a clear membership covenant, and persons can join our church and serve in the various offices of elder, deacon, etc., without changing their denomination. In this way we challenge one another to bring the best that the Holy Spirit is teaching us in our various denominational traditions and enrich one another.

Now as Jesus concludes this prayer, we are reminded again of the early verses of the Gospel (1:1–3). Jesus refers to His relationship with the Father in love "before the foundation of the world" (17:24). This relates directly to the opening words of the Gospel, "In the beginning was the Word...all things were made by him."

And the prayer closes with Jesus' summation of salvation—that we might know the Father through Him, and that God's love may be in us and Christ in us. Paul worded it this way when he wrote to the Colossian Christians, "Christ *in you*, the hope of glory" (Col. 1:27, italics mine).

Merciful Father, Help me to sow peace, love, joy, amongst Your believers even, and especially, in the face of schism and conflict. AMEN.

WHAT THIS SCRIPTURE MEANS TO ME—John 16–17

The first truth of this lesson for me is that the Holy Spirit is my divine Helper. Just as the function of my heart is to pump blood through my physical body, the Holy Spirit is the One who enables me to walk in the Spirit through the trials and testings that I experience.

He is my Helper on all assignments that are too big for me. But there is one time in particular when I experienced His help that comes to mind as if it were yesterday.

On the Friday evening before Easter of 1983 the young director of the Theatre Ministry in our church dropped a bomb in my lap as I sat beside him at a dinner party.

"Dorothy, how are you coming on 'The Hiding Place'?" (Months before he had asked me to adapt the book into a three-act play for a future dinner theatre production in our church.)

"Oh I haven't started on it yet, but I promise I'll get busy on it soon," I replied vaguely.

"Better make it sooner than soon," Steve said. "I've scheduled rehearsals to start the middle of May."

I don't remember anything else about the evening except how quickly it was ruined for me. My stomach was tied in knots; I broke out in perspiration. There was no way I could write the adaptation in time. I was upset with Steve for not telling me months before that he expected to cast the play in May. And I was upset with myself for my lack of discipline.

Driving home that evening my husband said to me, "Dorothy, you seem unusually quiet. Is something bothering you?"

"Yes, something is. Steve told me that he has scheduled rehearsals to begin on 'The Hiding Place' in less than a month. I haven't even started on it. Charles, you know that I can't write a three-act play in so short a time. It's impossible to work at home with so many necessary interruptions. Besides, I've got an out-of-town speaking engagement next week."

"No you don't, Dorothy. You don't have anything on for next week. I looked at your calendar just before we left to be sure of the time of this dinner. The rest of the month hardly has a free day, but you have nothing written on your calendar at all for the next week. Why don't you pack a few things in a bag and fly up to our house in Colorado? With no phone to bother you and no one knowing you're coming, you could have a whole week of uninterrupted work." He reached over and squeezed my hand, "Besides, I'd enjoy a quiet week with a couple of good books I've been wanting to read."

The day after Easter I flew to Colorado.

I've never known such a week. In the quiet of that beautiful little vacation house we call "Hethlon" (The Hebrew word for "a hiding place") and with the fellowship of my Lord in the person of His Holy Spirit, I wrote the adaptation. Although His power is not always discernible experientially, I was continually aware of His presence. Scenes that wouldn't mesh at bedtime would be worked out easily the next morning. The Divine Helper was with me guiding me into all truth just as Jesus had promised He would (John 16:13). When I flew home seven days later, the adaptation was all written with the exception of a couple of short scene revisions. Rehearsals began on schedule. The Holy Spirit had indeed been my helper.

The second truth in this study for me is the joy that Jesus promises us that cannot be taken away. He likens it to the joy of a mother who has just given birth. She doesn't remember the pain, but cradling that new life in her arms is unforgettable.

Nothing can ever take away the joy that I experienced that week in Colorado. I wasn't too keen on being by myself for a whole week. I'd never done that before, but the quiet and the peace left no place for the fear of being alone that I had experienced all my life. Whenever I recall those days, a new joy bubbles up that I have no words for. It is a spiritual joy. It is the gift of the Spirit.

The final truth for me found in this study is in the priestly prayer that Jesus prayed for His disciples during their last hours together before His death. And I know that He prayed this prayer for me too—He says so in the twentieth verse. In this prayer Jesus prayed that we would be one as He and the Father are one, and finally "that the love wherewith thou didst love me may be in them and I in them."

What wonderful promises we have in this study. The promise that the Holy Spirit will live in us and be our Helper; the assurance that in Jesus our joy is complete; and the greatest truth of all: "Jesus loves me this I know."

He is on our side!

LESSON 7
JOHN 18–19

Christ the Reconciler—in Love

Father God, Teach me to serve You with Christlike conviction. Edify me with Your Word. AMEN.

Love is a depth of caring that opens one's life fully to that of another. We read earlier in our Gospel account that God so loved the world that He gave His only begotten Son. That kind of love calls for a response of love on our part. We love Him because He first loved us. And now, because we are His disciples, His love is poured into our lives through the Holy Spirit (Rom. 5:5). If love was possible without the gospel, we wouldn't need the gospel. On the other hand, if love is not possible through the gospel, we have no gospel. But the truth is that love is made possible by the gospel, and that is what Christian discipleship is all about!

John tells us now that when the meal was over Jesus and His disciples left the upper room and walked the short distance across the brook Kedron to the Garden of Gethsemane, a place they often frequented. One can't help but wonder why Jesus didn't go someplace where He wouldn't be so easily found since He knew He was going to be betrayed and arrested. But authentic love doesn't run. Rather, it participates in love without reacting to the way it's treated. Jesus' kind of love could confront hostility without becoming hostile in return (18:1–11). In fact, the depth of Jesus' love is seen in His suffering and death.

Love—that Doesn't Resist.

119

How far short of this most of us come. It is easier to respond to anger with anger, to violence with violence. Turning the other cheek, being free to respond differently from the way in which we have been treated, takes an inner strength from God's grace. Yet this is the Christian's strategy of operation.

John relates Judas' betrayal by fully identifying him with the enemies of Jesus. Judas was a child of this world and he failed to embrace the kingdom of God which Jesus announced. By betraying Jesus he chose the way of coercion and violence rather than the Way of freedom and love seen in Jesus.

Jesus' composure, courage, and boldness before the mob was a reflection of His own inner peace and authority (18:4–8). He knew who He was, and one who stands in truth and love is not vulnerable before deceit and violence.

In this scene John does not report on Judas' act of identifying Jesus with a kiss, but instead he lets us see Jesus' fearless demeanor before the mob. They had been led to the Garden of Gethsemane by Judas. He knew that this part of the garden was Jesus' place of prayer and rest. It was here that the dramatic confrontation took place, and as Jesus identified Himself, John writes that the mob fell back to the earth (18:6), a sign of the power Jesus had—a power that could have been used for His escape had He so chosen. But love does not run from trouble, and Jesus' selfless love was expressed in His appeal that the mob would let His disciples alone (18:8).

Next John describes Peter's impulsive action. He drew his sword and cut off the ear of the high priest's servant, Malchus. John takes particular care to tell us it was his "right ear." This could mean that Peter was a poor swordsman, or that the servant turned his head at just the right moment, or perhaps Peter was left-handed. One wonders at the specificity, except that it relates the story in a simplistic form. But of far more importance is Jesus' rebuke to Peter, "Put up thy sword into the sheath: the cup which my Father hath given me, shall I not drink it?" (18:11). Jesus made it clear that He was completely submissive to the Father's will.

On one of his Thracian campaigns, Julius Caesar captured Spartacus the gladiator. He sent him to the arena to fight an unknown opponent. As Spartacus entered the arena, he spoke a phrase that was peculiar to the area where his boyhood home was located. In a flash his opponent responded with an equally familiar phrase. Suddenly Spartacus realized he was standing toe to toe with his younger brother! He threw his short sword across the arena, reached out and jerked the helmet from his brother's head, and kissed him on the cheek. Calling out to Caesar he said, "Sir, we fight not, for we are brothers." As Christians reconciled in love with our brothers and sisters across the world, our response to the people and situations in life is to be like that of Jesus in the garden—boldly determined in peace to do the Father's will.

In writing about Peter's militant action in the garden that night, Matthew tells us that Jesus described an important principle of Christian behavior when He said to Peter, "Put up your sword... for all they that take the sword shall perish with the sword" (Matt. 26:52). In the sixteenth century, when the Swiss Reformer, Huldrich Zwingli went to war against the Catholics to defend his cause, he was killed on the battlefield. Martin Luther, upon hearing of the death of his friend, quoted these same words, "They that take the sword shall perish with the sword."

It was there in the garden among the olive trees that night under the full moon of the Passover just hours before His death that Jesus showed us the *better way*—the way of life and victory.

Love—under Test.

The trial of Jesus was really the exposure of the human family (18:12–27). To reject such a One as Jesus of Nazareth meant a choice for evil against God. And the choice was made by the Jewish religious community as well as by the secular/political community. This is highlighted by the fact that Jesus was taken before both Annas, retired high priest, and then to his son-in-law, Caiaphas, the then current high priest (18:13–14).

On a particularly meaningful occasion my wife Esther and I were in the British Art Museum in London, enjoying the paintings of the great masters. As we left one room to enter another, we were confronted by the Hornhurst painting of Jesus before Caiaphas. In this magnificent art masterpiece we saw Jesus, the Son of God, standing bound in front of this puny and sinister man who has the audacity to shake his finger in the face of Christ. The contrast between the two is a sight we will never forget—here artistically represented before us was good and evil.

Ancient steps climbing from the Kidron Valley up which Jesus was led after His arrest.

The Church of St. Peter in Gallicantu (cock's crow) in Jerusalem.
This is located over the traditional site of the House of the High Priest
where Jesus was taken after His arrest in the Garden of Gethsemane.

John makes special note of the prediction given by Caiaphas to the Jewish leaders, "...it was expedient that one man should die for the people" (18:14), a repeat of a prophecy he had made earlier (11:51). Most certainly these words originated not from his piety but by virtue of his position. Here is a prime example of the kind of person who has a head knowledge of religion but is totally lacking in spiritual and moral perception.

We are told next that Peter and "another disciple" followed Jesus to the high priest's house. Tradition holds that this other disciple was John who was apparently acquainted with the high priest and had access into his palace. Such being the case it appears clear that this detailed account of the events told here is not secondhand, and it also tells us something about John's social acceptance in Jerusalem society. It is thought that Zebedee had a house in Jerusalem from which he marketed salt fish and supplied the house of Caiaphas. Peter's easy access was due to John's friendship, as it was John who interceded with the maid at the door and secured Peter's entrance to the palace itself (18:15–16).

The stories of Peter's denial and of Jesus' interrogation are interspersed in John's account of what happened. In this we see a sharp contrast between Peter's weakness and Jesus' strength. As the high priest asked Jesus about His disciples and His doctrine (18:19–21), the two visible aspects of His program and influence, Jesus answered fearlessly and directly. And when one of the officers took exception to the directness of Jesus' response, he "struck Jesus with the palm of his hand..."(18:22) even though He was bound (18:24). In turn Jesus gave a bold rebuke to the officer who struck him (18:23). We see in Jesus' words and actions here that love is not weak, and it does hold people accountable.

The account of Peter's denial of Jesus (18:17–18; 25–27) exposes not only Peter's weakness, but ours as well and our tendency to self-preservation at any cost. Many of us meet ourselves in Peter. So often we find ways to compromise for self-interest rather than to accept the cost of love. The late Dr. E. Stanley Jones, prominent missionary and preacher, mentioned three basic areas of temptation; the self drive, the social drive, and the sex drive. In the story of Peter's denial it is possible that all three of these converged in one experience. Peter denied his Lord—the most important person in his life—under the social and self-preservation pressures of the young women servants of the palace and of the soldiers who had arrested Jesus.

Compromise tends to accelerate. Peter's first denial made the second become more emphatic, and the third was accompanied by an oath. It is possible that John's respect for his erring friend may well be reflected in the matter-of-fact, nonjudgmental way in which he tells the story.

John doesn't give us the final scene of Peter's denial. But you will recall in our study of Luke that as soon as the cock crowed "the Lord turned, and looked upon Peter" (Luke 22:61), and that loving look accomplished far more than any reprimand, for "Peter went out, and wept bitterly" (Luke 22:62). This marks the difference between Peter and Judas. The latter would not repent and come back to the Master.

Love is not a guarantee that we won't fail at times, but when we're put to the test, love does call us back.

We come now to Jesus' infamous civil trial before Pilate, the Roman governor (18:28–40). While the conniving Jewish religious leaders were determined to see Jesus killed, we find a touch of irony in verse 28 because they refused to enter Pilate's judgment hall—in so doing they would have become "defiled" religiously. They had no scruples about manipulating events and stories so as to kill an innocent man, but they didn't want to break one of their "religious" rules.

Love—that Faces the Powers.

Pilate didn't want to deal with Jesus (18:33–38). He wanted Jesus off his hands. But the leaders from the Sanhedrin made it clear that their "kangaroo court" wanted Jesus put to death. The verdict was already given—they only needed Pilate to authorize the execution. That's why they'd brought Jesus to the Fortress of Antonia to be tried by the Roman governor.

The interchange between Pilate and Jesus contains one of the most striking presentations in the Gospel. It is before the political authority that Jesus clearly states His kingship and the nature of His kingdom. It is a kingdom of love, of freedom, of truth. It is a kingdom of peace, for Jesus said, "My kingdom is not of this world: if my kingdom were of this world, then would my servants fight" …(18:36). He wanted Pilate, the man of political authority and power, to know that He was talking about the kingdom of God, not an earthly realm.

Pilate's response to Jesus' witness to Truth was typical of the agnostic mind; "What is truth?" (18:38). In other words who can be sure? How can we know? And yet the One who stood before him had said earlier, "I am the way, the truth, and the life: no one cometh unto the Father, but by me" (14:6). If we would know the truth of God, we must be open to be confronted by God! We can't handle the truth of God as an idea, or it is not the Truth of God. A person can be known only in relationship.

Truth aims to teach people how to take sides. Truth is not neutrality, rather it produces the boldest and bravest of spirits. In Christ God took sides—for us! And as Christians, as children of God, we can never back away from the responsibility of making spiritual decisions.

That Pilate could recognize authentic claims is seen in his attempt to negotiate Jesus' release (18:39). Significantly, here and on three other occasions Pilate said, "I find in him no fault at all" (18:38). His offer to release a prisoner was an attempt to get Jesus off, and the comparison of Jesus with Barabbas was a contrast between peace and violence, love and hostility, faith and force, service and theft. But the mob's choice of Barabbas (18:40) revealed the full character of their hostility, for their antagonism toward the Messiah and their desire to secure their own place of power was of the very spirit of Barabbas. They chose the kingdom of the world rather than the kingdom of God.

Love—that Accepts Rejection.

The Creed of the Apostles reads, "...suffered under Pontius Pilate, was crucified..." Our Scripture lesson now gives us in graphic terms the account of Jesus' complete rejection by the Jerusalem mob (19:1–16). First, Jesus is tied to the whipping post to be scourged—Roman torture intended to weaken a victim before crucifixion. The scourging itself was done with a whip of leather thongs with metal barbs which lacerated the flesh. Many persons collapsed under such scourging. In Jesus' case the whipping was accompanied by the mockery of the soldiers who pressed a crown of thorns into His head and dressed Him in a purple robe. And this was followed by jeers and slaps and punches as they taunted Him about being King of Jews (19:2–3).

Pilate's act of bringing the scourged, thorn-crowned Jesus out to the people was no doubt an attempt to satisfy the crowd that Jesus had been beaten. Stating again that he found no fault in Him, Pilate called upon the crowd to "Behold the man," hoping to now release Him (19:4–5). But the cry of the crowd, stirred up by the leaders, was "Crucify him" (19:6). What a contrast to the welcome given Him just a few days before, when Jesus had entered Jerusalem to the tumultuous cries, "Hosanna to the Son of David."

Now the accusation took up a new note, "...he made himself the Son of God" (19:7). It is significant that Pilate did not mock at this, but took it seriously. He had been impressed by Jesus' person and presence. John writes, "...he was the more afraid" (19:8). Even after all of this Pilate took the beaten Jesus into the judgment hall and asked again who He was! And when Jesus didn't answer, Pilate tried to move Him to answer by a reference to his own Roman power (19:10).

In response to Pilate's assertion of power Jesus now answered that He knew only one Power—the power of God—and all other power was only that granted by God (19:11). In writing to the Roman Christians Paul picks up on this same theme when he says, "For there is no power but of God: the powers that be are ordained of God" (Rom. 13:1). God is always above the powers of this world.

The extent of the treachery and madness of the Jewish religious leaders is revealed now in how they respond to Pilate's effort to release the innocent Jesus. They, in so many words, blackmail him by saying he would be disloyal to Caesar if he let Jesus go (19:12). His tenure as governor had been marked by disastrous failure, but a charge of disloyalty to his emperor would have ruined him, so he caved in. Then after another scene in the judgment hall Pilate stood Jesus before the mob and said, "Behold your King" (19:14).

The depth to which the Jewish leaders had sunk surfaces now as they shout back at Pilate, "We have no king but Caesar" (19:15). Their hatred of Roman rule was no secret, and Pilate must have been amazed at their duplicity. They had always proclaimed that God was their only king, but now in the heat of this black moment they had made their choice—it was the kingship of Caesar rather then the kingdom of God. And in making this choice they had rejected the King of Kings.

Matthew tells us that even as the mob was demanding Jesus' death, Pilate called for a basin of water and washed his hands in front of the crowd as a symbol that he was not responsible for the death of an innocent man, but in their madness the crowd accepted that responsibility with their shouts of "crucify him." They chose the way of Barabbas and rejected the way of Jesus.

It is easy for us to be critical of the mob that condemned Jesus. We're too civilized to condone a barbarous act of crucifixion and murder. And yet we so often stand aside and compromise the truth. But this same Jesus stands by in love and waits for us to confess Him as Lord (Rom. 10:9–10).

Love—that Bears Our Sins.

Crucifixion is the most horrible death conceivable. Originally a Persian method, it was taken up by the Romans as a way of executing criminals. The pubic display of the agony of a person crucified may have been seen as a deterrent to other criminals. The victim was nailed to the cross by spikes driven through the base of the hands. The weight of the body would then cause the victim to sag until the lung cage collapsed. And then, fighting for breath the dying person would press down on his feet in an effort to straighten up in a struggle for air. For many, death came slowly, and the torture dragged on for hours.

Jesus was put to death in this cruel way. Peter writes, "Who his own self bare our sins in his own body on the tree, that we being dead to sins, should live unto righteousness: by whose stripes ye were healed" (1 Pet. 2:24). Jesus literally carried in Himself the full brunt of our sin, absorbing our hostility to the death, while at the same time assuring us of forgiveness.

It was customary to have the condemned man carry his own cross (19:17). Weakened and lacerated from the scourging the victim would stumble along the way, goaded on by the soldiers. One soldier would usually walk ahead of the condemned person carrying the placard naming the offense. In the case of Jesus the sign read "Jesus of Nazareth, the king of the Jews" (19:19).

Jesus was crucified at Golgotha, the place of the skull, evidently a small rounded hill outside the city wall that was shaped something like a skull. It was near the city, and as people passed by they could read the inscription, written in Hebrew, Greek, and Latin (19:20). The chief priests asked Pilate to change the wording, but he refused. On this, Pilate stood firm.

It was customary also for the soldiers who were on duty at an execution to divide among themselves the few things

Gordon's Calvary. A skull-shaped hill identified by many scholars as the likely place where Jesus was crucified.

the crucified person owned. Traditionally, these consisted of five articles—shoes, turban, girdle, tunic, and an outer robe. John tells us that Jesus' tunic was a seamless robe and the soldiers threw dice to see which one would have it (19:24).

The cross very early became a symbol adopted by the followers of Jesus to represent His atoning death. The mosaic cross pictured here is from a recently excavated chapel in southern Israel built in the early Christian centuries.

And John also refers to the action of the soldiers as being in fulfillment of the prophecy in Psalm 22:18, "They part my garments among them, and cast lots upon my vesture."

Love—that Gives Its Life.

Crucifixion allowed for some expressions from the dying Saviour that another sudden death would have prevented. John himself was near the cross (19:26), witnessing the sordid event. And there were four women standing near the cross, including Jesus' mother, Mary. Imagine, if you can, Mary's feelings as she followed Jesus to His death and remembered all of God's promises to her about her son. Also present was Jesus' aunt, Salome, Mary the wife of Clopas, and Mary of Magdala whom he had delivered from demonic powers (19:25). The faithfulness of these women is a testimony to the meaningful relationships Jesus had with them throughout all His ministry (Luke 8:2–3).

John includes the amazing tender scene in which Jesus, in the midst of His agony, attends to the needs of His mother. He commissions John to become a son in His place and care for Mary, and He calls Mary's attention to the new relationship: "Woman, behold thy son" (19:26), a statement that assured her of John's care.

We are told next in verse 28 that Jesus knew that everything had been accomplished, and then He cried, "I thirst." I believe two things are implied here. First, thirst meant that the agony of the cross was genuine, for intense thirst accompanied crucifixion; second, Jesus did not think of His own need, His thirst, until after He knew that His atoning work was completed. The reference to giving Jesus vinegar on a sponge affixed to a hyssop branch (19:29) reminds us of the first Passover in Egypt when hyssop was used to put blood on the doorposts and on the lintel as a sign of their deliverance.

John then records Jesus' death cry as a shout of victory, "It is finished" (19:30). The Greek word, *tetelestai*, was the cry of victory or achievement. Soldiers used it when they took a city, herdsmen used it when they saw the results of careful animal husbandry, and artists used it when they'd completed a painting. Salvation was now finished. Jesus had faced all of Satan's antagonism and temptations, and He was victor. Satan's opposition was carried to the ultimate, to Jesus' death, but while they crushed Jesus' body they couldn't crush His spirit!

And John makes it clear that Jesus died, "...he bowed

his head, and gave up the ghost" (19:30). This was in turn attested to by the soldiers who came to break the legs of the men on the crosses— done to quicken death because it kept them from pushing up to get their breath. The soldiers didn't break Jesus' legs because they saw He was already dead. He had given His life! One of the soldiers took his lance and pierced Jesus' side, puncturing the heart area. John says that water and blood flowed out— the water added to the blood was an indication of the intense suffering He endured at His death.

Socrates said, "God may forgive sin, but I don't see how he can." The Good News of the gospel is that Jesus forgives at the deepest cost to Himself. He died in my place, in our place. Calvary reveals the intensity of our sin against Him. But Calvary expresses the depth of His love for us. We have redemption through His blood.

Love—that Died for Us All.   The Apostle's Creed states, "He was crucified, dead, and buried." The account of Jesus' burial is witness to the fact that He actually died (19:38–42). From the Gnostics to the followers of Islam, there have been those who question whether Jesus as the Son of God could actually die. Attempts have been made to distinguish between spirit and body in an effort to say that the divine in Jesus of Nazareth could not die. But the Incarnation, as presented in Scripture, tells us of Jesus the Christ who died for us. Paul, in writing to the Philippian Christians said that this Jesus, "Who being in the form of God...was made in the likeness of men...and became obedient unto death, even the death of the cross" (Phil. 2:6–8).

Next, in describing Jesus' burial, John tells us that two men are involved: Joseph of Arimathaea and Nicodemus, both dissenting members of the Sanhedrin that had condemned Jesus to death (19:38–39). But these two were secret disciples of Jesus. Before His death they had kept their belief with modest reserve, but upon His death they came forward to render a special service to Him in a fitting Jewish burial. Joseph provided his own tomb, and Nicodemus brought the spices and linen clothes to shroud the corpse.

As we review the story, it would seem that these men could have openly supported Jesus in life as a better expression of faith than to serve Him after death. Yet we applaud their gracious act. And we may conclude that the impact of Jesus' death had a greater influence upon them than had His life.

The day of crucifixion was also the day of preparation for the special sabbath, special in its association with the Passover. At the very time the priest was sacrificing the Passover lamb, the Lamb of God died on the cross! And as evening approached, it was Jewish law that the body should be taken down and buried before sabbath began at 6:00 p.m. Joseph and Nicodemus completed this rite as they placed Him in a "new sepulchre, wherein was never man yet laid" (19:41).

The descent from the cross has been the theme of innumerable paintings by artists of many cultures, and it was the theme of Michaelangelo's magnificent *Pietàs*. Among these is one less known than the famous *Pietà* in Rome. It is the *Pietà* in Florence in which Nicodemus is holding the body of Christ in place of Mary, and Michaelangelo placed his own face on Nicodemus. This witness by the artist calls us to identify with Christ in His death, for with Paul we must say, "I am crucified with Christ: nevertheless I live; yet not I, but Christ liveth in me: and the life which I now live in the flesh I live by the faith of the Son of God, who loved me, and gave himself for me" (Gal. 2:20).

Carroll S. Ringgold tells a story which involved a white cross on the side of a hill outside of a large city. It seems that a little boy was lost in the city and a policeman tried in vain to help him find his way home. Finally the little boy said, "Take me to the cross on the hill, and I can find my way from there!"

Abba, Father, Help me to daily appreciate my new life in You—I'm sometimes tempted to take it for granted. Give me a fresh vision of Calvary. AMEN.

WHAT THIS SCRIPTURE MEANS TO ME—John 18–19

The ugliest event in the history of the world took place in Jerusalem that day when Jesus Christ, the only begotten Son of God, was executed on a cross between two thieves.

The Cross seemed to be the worst defeat the little band of disciples could ever know, but it would be turned into the greatest victory the world has ever known. Jesus Christ's victory over death has been bequeathed to each of us who are believers in Him. We can say with Paul "Oh death where is thy sting? Oh grave where is thy victory?" (I Cor. 15:55).

John's account of the arrest and trial and crucifixion of Jesus differs in some instances from the other Gospels. John identifies Peter as the one who cut off the ear of the High Priest's servant, and he gives the servant a name—Malchus. This had to be a miracle that the servant would never forget. I've often wondered if he ever became a believer. Why else would John want us to know his name?

A well-known writer tells about the time the small volunteer fire department in her town was called to put out the fire of a car burning on the highway. The writer's husband and a young minister were two of the volunteers. Before they could reach the fire the car was incinerated and five people lost their lives.

Returning home after the tragedy the young minister lashed out at God in anguish, "Where were you? Where were you, God?"

And the writer quietly replied, "In the fire."

Two thousand years ago on the cross of Calvary Jesus experienced the fire along with the pain and the anguish of this hurt and sick and dying world.

He felt the pangs of the millions who go to bed each night hungry.

He bore the suffering of the abused child.

He experienced the agony of Russian believers imprisoned in the Gulags that abound in that dark midnight country. When Georgi Vins (one of the five Russian dissidents exchanged for two Russian spies during President Carter's term in office) was asked why he was sentenced to prison, he replied, "Because I wrote the 23rd Psalm." Then smiling he said, "I do write poetry, but my authorship of the 23rd Psalm is certainly going to surprise King David."

Jesus carried on the cross the grief of that young friend of mine whose husband had a heart attack and died before she could even say good-bye.

And He bore on the cross the suffering of my friend Edith. Edith was a stately woman. With her hair piled high on her head she carried her slender body with the elegance of a princess. Edith had class. She also had cancer.

One time she said to me, "I do not understand it, but I feel that Jesus is as close as my breath, encouraging me, assuring me that His grace is sufficient for my every need. I know that He has already been through all that I am experiencing. I feel strange even saying it but I know that the reason I can have such inner peace is because His overcoming joy has been given to me. I've had all the treatment I can have. And the elders of the church have anointed me with oil and prayed for my healing. But I've already been healed emotionally and spiritually and that is much more important than this physical body."

Jesus took Edith home to heaven on the Saturday after Thanksgiving. Just four hours before her death she and I sang her favorite song, "Jesus, Name Above All Names." Then she asked my husband about his tennis partner, a young man who had recently been diagnosed as having leukemia—she had recently been praying for him.

There was no sting in Edith's death, just the peace that passes all understanding. She knew that Jesus paid it all on the cross at Calvary and that she would be with Him forever. Death was conquered for her and for all of us almost two thousand years ago.

LESSON 8
JOHN 20–21

Christ the Reconciler— in Hope

Father, Your Word admonishes me to "glory in understanding and knowing You." Use this lesson to further my knowledge of You, Lord. AMEN.

The resurrection of Jesus is the pivotal point of Christian faith. While the triumph of Jesus was on the cross, without the empty tomb the victory of the cross could have been fruitless. Paul summed it up for the Roman Christians by writing that Jesus "...was delivered for our offenses, and was raised again for our justification" (Rom. 4:25). It is in His life that we live. His resurrection victory is our hope, and hope is acting in faith that His victory is timeless.

Hope—in the Empty Tomb.

The other Gospels tell us that Mary Magdalene and several other women came early to the tomb the first day of the week, intending to complete the burial treatment of the body to fulfill Jewish embalming rites. John refers only to Mary who went very early to the tomb while it was still dark and found to her surprise that the stone was rolled away (20:1). John then adds that Mary ran immediately to the city and reported to Peter and "the other disciple whom Jesus loved," John himself, that "They have taken

The Garden Tomb, adjacent to Gordon's Calvary where many believe Jesus was buried. The stone channel in which a large stone would be rolled to seal the opening of the tomb can be seen.

The grounds adjacent to the Garden Tomb. Christian groups gather here each Sunday morning to worship the resurrected Saviour.

away the Lord out of the sepulchre, and we know not where they have laid him" (20:2).

Upon receiving that shocking news the two men ran to the garden to investigate Mary's story. The younger John outran Peter, and when he arrived at the tomb he stood at the door looking in. But when Peter came up, he went right into the tomb and then John followed. They saw the linen clothes lying neatly in the grave, and the napkin that had been used to wrap Jesus' head, perhaps binding the lower jaw, was folded in place separate from the shroud (20:3–7).

John then testifies to the fact that when he saw the empty shroud in the deserted sepulchre, he became a believer in the resurrection of our Lord (20:8). Even with all that Jesus had said about His death and resurrection on earlier occasions the disciples still didn't understand. So we have to ask: what did John believe at this point? It is difficult to say, but it must have been the dawning of faith. And yet, John now tells us that the two men left that awesome scene and "went away again unto their own home" (20:10). That sounds pretty routine and matter-of-fact. There wasn't apparently any of the resurrection joy and zeal that later turned them into bold witnesses. Evidently the empty grave wasn't enough; they had to meet the risen Lord.

Faith by its very nature is a response to evidence, and these disciples now needed to process the evidence. At the same time we, too, need to look at the evidence. The tomb is empty, the Lord is not there; He is risen. But we today have the benefit of almost 2,000 years of Christian witness—the changed lives of hundreds of thousands of people who have met the risen Christ in faith is evidence that the Lord is active in our world. We need to acknowledge Him, open ourselves to His presence, and realize that we are never alone. Jesus is with us—now!

Hope—in the Risen One.

The first person to see the risen Christ was Mary Magdalene (20:11–18). This is one of the most moving stories of the Bible. Mary had come early to the tomb, and as we have just read, when she saw that the stone had been pushed aside, she ran to tell Peter and John.

Apparently, Mary returned to the tomb and arrived there after Peter and John had left. After grieving for her lost Lord for a time outside the sepulchre, she stooped down and looked inside (20:11). It was then that she saw the two angels who asked why she was crying. After explaining her great sense of loss, she turned back into the garden, and through her tears she saw a man standing there whom she presumed was the gardener. In desperation she asked, "Sir, if thou have borne him hence, tell me where thou hast laid him, and I will take him away" (20:15).

The next moment presents the greatest scene of recognition in the resurrection stories. The man standing there, Jesus Himself, spoke her name, "Mary," in a tone that she immediately recognized, and she cried out, "Rabboni," a word in Aramaic that recognizes the divine in the teacher! Literally, Mary cried out, "My Lord!" This was her great confession as she fell at His feet (20:16).

Evidentally, Mary had grasped Jesus' feet, for He said, "Touch me not; for I am not yet ascended to my Father..." (20:17). Again Jesus refers to the coming event mentioned earlier in His prayer (Chapter 17) when He was preparing the disciples for His return to the Father. Now He tells Mary the same thing and then He adds, "...go to my brethren, and say unto them, I ascend unto my Father, and your Father; and to my God, and your God" (20:17). What a powerful message of reconciliation and hope for the questioning and confused disciples—and for us. Through Jesus, His Father and His God is *our* Father and *our* God.

Mary now became the first witness of the resurrection. This may be seen as adding credibility to the witness, for it did not come first from one of the twelve disciples. Or it may be seen as Jesus' confirmation of the importance of women, as well as men, among His disciples. Mary then ran to tell the disciples that she had seen the Lord and talked with Him. Now it was not only the empty tomb which Peter and John had as evidence of Jesus' resurrection, but the witness of one who had seen Jesus and knew beyond a doubt that He was alive—He is risen!

Dr. Leslie Newbigin tells the story of a Russian Communist leader, Bukharin, who led an anti-God rally in Kiev in the 1920s. At the conclusion of his speech an Orthodox priest came forward and asked permission to say a few words. When he stepped to the podium, he gave clearly and joyfully the Christian greeting, "Christ is risen." From the vast crowd there came back as with one great voice, "He is risen indeed!"

Hope—in Peace for All.

The post-resurrection appearances of Jesus are variously reported by the Gospel writers. John includes several accounts not reported in the other three Gospels, even as the others describe some that John omits. We are told by Luke of Jesus' appearance to two people as they walked on the road to Emmaus. And then, after these two discovered who their fellow traveler really was, they hurried back, and learned from their friends that Jesus was alive and had appeared to Peter. It was later that evening that Jesus appeared to the disciples—the story John now tells us (20:19–23).

John writes that the disciples were behind closed doors

for fear of the Jews. How often our fears cause us to withdraw, to hide behind our masks, to seek protection in our limited securities. We next read that suddenly Jesus stood among them, and said, "Peace be unto you" (20:19)— *Shalom* in Hebrew. This is the abiding greeting of God's grace. It was a common greeting in Jesus' day, and it has also lived through the centuries to the present time.

Jesus followed the greeting by showing the disciples His hands and his side (20:20). These were the three main wounds from the cross, and were the evidence that they were really seeing their crucified and risen Lord. The joy of the disciples was the expression of their dawning faith. Again Jesus said, "Peace be unto you" (20:21).

The next phrase,"...as my Father hath sent me, even so send I you," remind us of the great commission, and are almost a direct quotation from His prayer in 17:18. Jesus was sending His disciples out in a ministry of reconciliation, a ministry of the same nature as His own reconciling ministry.

Dr. E. Stanley Jones, missionary statesman to India, told about a visit with Ghandi in which he asked, "What should I do? I am an American Christian missionary; do you want me to go home?" Ghandi replied, "No, but live your religion, be clear about what you believe, make love primary, and be more understanding of other religions." This is a great four-point mission strategy as we carry out Jesus' commission in today's world.

In verse 22 we are given what seems like a pre-pentecost Pentecost when Jesus said, "Receive ye the Holy Ghost." However, the problem of relating this to the event in Acts 2 can be resolved by noting that the Greek language here is imperative, a command. It could well read, "You *must* receive the Holy Spirit." And while this particular account in John gives no further explanation, we can readily conclude that Jesus' command became a reality several weeks later on the Day of Pentecost. John's reporting of this command of Jesus corresponds to the instructions in Luke 24:49, where the disciples were told by Jesus to stay in Jerusalem until they received the Holy Spirit.

Jesus then closed this dialogue with the disciples by declaring that the privilege of telling people that their sins are forgiven, or the responsibility to hold the unrepentant accountable, is a work of the Holy Spirit (20:23). We can serve God in this way only when we are operating in His presence under the anointing of the Spirit.

Hope—in Answers to Doubt.

The expression "A doubting Thomas" is used frequently. Recently I heard a commercial on T.V. for automobiles that began, "Don't be a doubting Thomas." It is from the story John tells us now that this expression comes (20:24–31). But perhaps we've been unfair in labeling Thomas this way. As a careful and logical thinker, he may have simply been asking for evidence.

The story says that Thomas, the twin (thought by some to have been the twin of Matthew), was not present that first evening when Jesus appeared. When he was told that the risen Lord had visited with the disciples and had showed them His hands and His side, Thomas made what I would call a normal response, "Except I shall see...I will not believe" (20:25). But we also read that "seeing" wouldn't be quite enough, for Thomas said that he would believe when he could put his finger into the print of the nails and his hand into the wound in Jesus' side. It is the intensity and detail of his statement that indicates the extent to which Thomas needed to be convinced.

John then describes a scene eight days later when the disciples, including Thomas, were together once again and suddenly, without warning, Jesus came into the room through closed doors and greeted them with the same word of "Peace."

This time Jesus centered His attention on Thomas and picked up on Thomas' words of a week before when He said, "Reach hither thy finger, and behold my hands; and reach hither thy hand, and thrust it into my side..." (20:27). And then Jesus added words that easily could have been put this way, "Stop becoming disbelieving,"—a suggestion that doubt believed adds more doubt.

Thomas responded with his great confession of faith, "My Lord and my God!" He moved from unfaith to faith—the most that can occur in a person. Jesus' response to Thomas called for him to recognize that the highest form of faith is not tied to the senses, but is related to evidence in other forms (20:29).

Before moving on, I want to make a few observations on doubt. First, doubt is the normal function of the seeking and inquiring mind. As Christians, it is normal to doubt, to ask questions, to seek certainty. At the same time, though, an agnostic needs to be called to honest doubt, to question agnostic presuppositions in order to come to faith. Second, doubt is as much a matter of the heart or will as of the mind. The real issues are—do we want to know God and do we want God in our lives? Dr. A. T. Robertson, prominent New Testament scholar of a past generation, used to say that doubt is not necessarily a mark of intellectual superiority. And third, doubt, when honest, becomes as thoroughly convinced as it was questioning when the evidence is clear.

And John has written this Gospel as evidence (20:31). He selected from Jesus' life and ministry those words and events he was led to write that we "...might believe that Jesus is the Christ, the Son of God"; and that in so believing we "might have life through his name" (20:31).

A student at Columbia University in New York was being destroyed by doubt. In his condition of unfaith he began to live a life of reckless dissipation. After one particularly wild night that stretched well into Sunday morning, he aimlessly dropped into a church near his dorm. As the pastor called the congregation to prayer, the young man sat looking about unconcerned. Suddenly, he saw his favorite science professor in the congregation with his head reverently bowed in prayer. At that moment a wave of doubt swept over him—if his intellectual professor prayed, then he as a student should be open to God. For him, a praying professor provided the answer to his lack of faith.

There's an interesting postscript to this story. After completing his training, this young man went to India as a Christian missionary. Years later when he was home on furlough he looked up his now retired professor friend and told him the story of that Sunday morning and how it had influenced his life for Christ.

Hope—in Evidence of His Presence.

Jesus had told His disciples that after the resurrection He would meet them in Galilee (Matt. 26:32; Mark 16:7). Then to make certain they understood, the angel in the empty tomb on resurrection morning told "Mary Magdalene and the other Mary" to tell the disciples that He would meet them at the mountain in Galilee that He had designated. We may surmise that in their uncertainty about Jesus' resurrection they didn't leave at once because the first two appearances Jesus made to the disciples, which we have just studied, occurred in Jerusalem. We don't know the reason for the delay—it may have been travel plans or possibly Thomas had been away from Jerusalem for a few days. But whatever the cause, after Jesus' second appearance, they left Jerusalem and traveled to Galilee. John now tells us about Jesus' third visit with the disciples (21:1–14).

Peter had no doubt become impatient with sitting around waiting for the unknown and turned to the known, for he announced, "...I go a fishing." Six other disciples responded and went with him. In a pattern well understood by such veteran Galilean fishermen, they spent the night on the lake but with no success.

As the mist was lifting at early dawn, the figure of a man could be seen on the shore. The man asked if they had any fish, and they admitted their failure (21:5). Then the man called back and said, "Cast the net on the right side of the ship, and ye shall find" (21:6). Still not recognizing Jesus, they did what He said because it was not unusual for a person standing on the shore to see a school of fish not readily visible at the moment to men in a boat. The result was staggering. The nets were so full they weren't able of themselves to pull them in (21:6).

John then turned to Peter with the awareness of faith, "It is the Lord" (21:7). Peter, stripped to his loin cloth, grabbed his cloak and plunged into the water, hurrying to the shore to greet his Lord. When the other disciples arrived on shore, they discovered that Jesus already had built a fire and some fish were cooked and ready for their breakfast. Then at a word from Jesus Peter pulled up the net and added fish to the fire from their catch.

John now tells us that while they were eating the fish and bread Jesus had prepared for them, "None of the disciples durst ask him, who art thou? knowing that it was the Lord" (21:12). The act of eating with them was a certification of His person and a renewal of their relationship.

This story of the third appearance of the risen Christ to a group of the disciples demonstrates the reality of the resurrection. While some people might want to believe that Jesus' appearances in the room in Jerusalem were hallucinations or visions from the spirit world, this story points to the truth that the risen Christ was a real person, not a spirit or vision. The risen Christ acted and talked like the Jesus of Nazareth they had lived with for over three years. He ate with them in familiar fellowship. He made it clear that He was the same Jesus, risen from the grave, conqueror of death!

Belief in the bodily resurrection of Jesus Christ was the transforming faith that changed the disciples. When we meet them in the ministries recorded in the book of Acts they are boldly announcing the resurrection of Jesus and His reign as Lord of Lords.

Hope—in the Testing of Our Love.

One-on-one conversations hold us to the more direct values in communication. Following breakfast that morning Jesus turned to Peter for a personal conversation (21:15–19). He had met Peter earlier to assure him of His love and forgiveness. But now, this personal interview with Peter in the presence of the other disciples reinstated him with the group and recommissioned him for service.

Peter had denied his Lord three times, and now Jesus asked him three times about his love (21:15–17). In telling the story John uses two different Greek words which in English are translated "love." In Jesus' questions He uses the word *agape*—self-giving love. When Peter responds, he uses the word *phileo*—friendship love. This play on words may be exaggerated in our distinctions, and yet the difference is very significant.

First, Jesus asked, "Simon, son of Jonas, lovest thou me more than these?" The reference may have been to the fishing boats anchored nearby. We can't tell because we have no way of knowing the objects of Jesus' gesture. If so, He is calling Peter to a vocation that transcends occupation. On the other hand the reference may have been to the other disciples, for Peter had said earlier that even though everyone else might desert Him, he wouldn't. If so, Jesus is leading Peter to take his place with the other disciples— all of whom were dependent upon God's grace. Peter's answer was that he had great friendship-love for Jesus.

Next, Jesus asked, "Simon, Son of Jonas, lovest thou me?" (21:16). Again, Jesus uses the word *agape*. This time Jesus may have been pressing the issue of the nature of Peter's love. Or the question may have been focusing on the object of his love—do you love *me*? It may be that Jesus wanted Peter to see the difference between loving Him and loving himself. Again, Peter responded by using *phileo*—You know that I am your friend.

The third time that Jesus asked the question He used

Peter's word *phileo*, and asked, "Are you truly my friend?" (21:17). John writes that Peter was grieved over the third question, either because of Jesus' repeated questioning, or perhaps because Jesus now raised the question about his "friendship-love." Clearly Jesus pressed Peter to the point of full honesty, of full self-awareness. For then Peter burst out, "You know all things, you know that I am your friend."

To each of Peter's answers Jesus responded with a commission, "Feed my lambs," "Feed my sheep," and again, "Feed my sheep." We may conclude that the evidence of Peter's love would be his service in the vocation to which Christ was calling him—shepherding the church that would soon emerge. Love involves responsibility. Love means faithfulness. But it also means active service at a cost of one's self.

And loving service is a necessary corollary to loving proclamation. Social concern and evangelistic proclamation belong together. We cannot separate faith from works, verbal witness from action.

Jesus closes this dialogue with Peter by predicting Peter's future martyrdom. And then He adds one more time, "Follow me" (21:19). This Peter did, and as shepherd of the church, Peter wrote later, referring to his role and that of his colleagues, and us, as "under shepherds" awaiting the appearance of the "Chief Shepherd" (1 Pet. 5:2–4).

Hope—in the Testimony of His Word.

In these closing words (21:20–25) we get a clue that John, the writer of this Gospel, must have written with the help of others. The witness to the truth of his testimony (21:24) was no doubt made by those in Ephesus who assisted him in his writing. The Muratorian Canon (A.D. 180) tells us that others encouraged John to write this Gospel and assisted him.

After hearing what Jesus had said about his future (21:18), Peter, looked around and, seeing John nearby, asked, "...what shall this man do?" (21:21). In Jesus' response He seems to be saying that it doesn't matter what happens to John or anyone else. Instead, it was important for Peter to remain faithful and in submission to his Master.

By the wording of Jesus' response, "If I will that he tarry till I come, what is that to thee," was evidently interpreted by some to mean that John would not die. This misconception is corrected as John tells us what Jesus actually said

(21:23). John wanted to be sure that the record was set straight.

But the important thing in verse 22 are the words, "...till I come." The promise of His second coming is simple and direct just as it had been throughout all of His teaching ministry. It is only His later interpreters that have added complexities to this great truth.

Now, as John comes to the end of his Gospel (21:25), having selected words and events from Christ's life, death, and resurrection to express the "Good News," he seems reluctant to conclude. His closing statement is witness to the greatness of our Lord and the extent of His revelation. John says that if everything Jesus did was recorded "I suppose that even the world itself could not contain the books that should be written." Actually, John is expressing his faith in the limitless meaning of the knowledge of God in Jesus Christ.

As our study together draws to a close, I am reminded of the witness of William Charles Bordon who turned his back on a huge family fortune to go to China as a missionary. He got as far as Egypt where he contracted typhoid fever and died, a young man still in his twenties. His dedication to the Lord was expressed in these words, "No reserve, no retreat, and no regret." It is this indomitable spirit—the spirit of Peter and John, the Gospel writer,—that has opened up the testimony of God's Word in all time. John expressed it so well in the opening verses of the Gospel, "As many as received him, to them gave he power to become the sons of God, even to them that believe on his name" (1:12). This is the Good News of the gospel for everyone in all time. Our hope is in Jesus Christ—our mission is to live that hope so that people everywhere are drawn to the Saviour.

Lord God, Help me to "live that hope"—Your hope—that frees me to rejoice and be confident in You! AMEN.

WHAT THIS SCRIPTURE MEANS TO ME—John 20–21

Our last lesson closed with Joseph of Arimathea claiming the body of Jesus, and along with Nicodemus, placing His body in a new tomb not far from Golgotha.

Three years ago our family visited that little garden tomb where many believe Jesus was buried. It is gloriously different from the magnificent memorial tombs of Napoleon Bonaparte, Vladimir Lenin, and Ulysses S. Grant simply because the garden tomb is empty and has been since that first Easter morning. For almost two thousand years that empty tomb has proclaimed to all the world that Jesus is victor over death, the final enemy.

John in these closing chapters of his Gospel tells of only four appearances of our Lord after His resurrection. He appeared to Mary in her grief, to the disciples imprisoned in fear, to Thomas encompassed in doubt, and to Peter in his guilt.

Jesus' first appearance was soon after His resurrection. He appeared before Mary who was weeping outside the tomb. Jesus came to her and her grief was turned into unspeakable joy. He called her by name and gave her a job to do: "Go tell the others."

He is still coming to us today in our grief. Jesus came to my friend Mary Ellen on that Labor Day in 1965 when she crawled into the back seat of her car brokenhearted. She along with her husband and young son were driving to South Texas to claim the body of their older son who had been killed in a traffic accident. It had been just six weeks since his graduation from law school, and he had been married just a month.

As Mary Ellen sat immobile in shock, she was suddenly aware of a Presence and heard these words: "My grace is sufficient for you, Mary Ellen." She attended the memorial service for her son with her head held high. Anthony was with the Lord and the Lord was with her. Jesus had come to her when she desperately needed Him just as He had come to Mary Magdalene in the garden on that resurrection morning.

On the evening of that first Easter Jesus appeared to His disciples. They were behind locked doors, fear gripping their hearts. Their Master had been crucified, and they were fearful that the Jewish leaders might be hunting them down next.

But Jesus came and stood in their midst and said, "Peace be with you." He then commissioned them for service and breathed on them the Holy Spirit. They would never again be afraid that way again.

The Intercontinental Hotel in Geneva was an armed fortress that day in 1975 when my husband and I were on vacation with a group of former students from three Texas universities. Mr. Henry Kissinger and Mr. Andrei Gromyko were also guests in that hotel. When you stepped off the elevator on your floor, you looked into the cold eyes of armed guards, submachine guns mounted and ready.

The morning of our departure we were awakened three hours before the scheduled time and hurried to the airport. Mr. Gromyko and Mr. Kissinger were flying to Bern later that same day. Our chartered jet was parked next to Air Force II and the Russian Aeroflot that had brought the Soviet leader to Geneva. The airport had to be secured hours before the diplomats would depart. We were ordered to take off in a thunderstorm. As the plane lumbered down the runway, rain was falling in sheets accompanied by lightning and crackling thunder. My stomach was in knots and my knuckles were white. I was rigid with fear. "Lord, give me your peace," I prayed under my breath. Long before we were out of the storm I had experienced a peace that was inexplicable. Jesus had come to me just as He had to the disciples when they too were afraid for their lives.

Thomas has been immortalized as the doubter. When Jesus appeared to the disciples that resurrection evening Thomas wasn't present. When the others told him later about what had happened, he said he wouldn't believe it until he could feel the nail prints and the wound in Jesus' side. Eight days later Thomas was with the group and Jesus appeared again. This time Thomas had the opportunity to prove for himself the reality of Jesus' resurrection. Jesus didn't rebuke Thomas for his doubts, He simply came to him where he was and did away with those doubts forever. Thomas would now stake his life on the evidence that demanded a verdict; Jesus was as He had claimed—the Son of God.

The last appearance of Jesus recorded in the Gospel of John is to the disciples on the shore of the Sea of Galilee. But it is with Peter that John records a personal conversation and commission. Again there is no judgment on Jesus' part, for Peter had confessed his sin with heartbroken repentance and been forgiven by his Lord. But now He gives Peter his assignment, "Feed my sheep." It is the same loving Lord who calls each one of us, who never loses track of our comings and goings, and who reminds us over and over that we are His witnesses. And it is the same Lord who has commissioned us to KNOW Him, for we cannot be His witnesses unless we really know Him as Lord and Saviour and the power of His resurrection has invaded our lives.

As we look around and see the wonders of God's magnificent creation, we can't help but ask with the psalmist, "What is man that thou art mindful of him?" and yet it is the Lord of the universe who calls us individually and offers us a place in His plan. Our fears, our doubts, our grief, our guilt, our education or lack of it, our age or our sex, our color or social or economic position, are all things to be offered to God after we have first presented our bodies as a living sacrifice to Him.

For me, the wonder of it all is summed up in "the gospel within the gospel" found in John 3:16: "For God so loved the world that He gave His only begotten son that whosoever believeth in Him should not perish but have eternal life."

THE SPECIFIC MIRACLES OF JESUS IN THE GOSPEL OF JOHN

Jesus turns the water into wine at the wedding at Cana	2:1–11
Jesus heals the nobleman's son	4:46–54
Jesus heals the man at the Pool of Bethesda	5:1–16
The feeding of the 5,000	6:1–14
Jesus walks on the Sea of Galilee	6:15–21
Jesus heals the man born blind	9:1–41
Lazarus raised from the dead	11:1–44

THE SEVEN "I AM" STATEMENTS IN THE GOSPEL OF JOHN

I am the bread of life	6:35
I am the light of the world	8:12
I am the door	10:7
I am the good shepherd	10:11
I am the resurrection and the life	11:25
I am the way, the truth, and the life	14:6
I am the true vine	15:1

A HARMONY OF THE GOSPELS

	MATTHEW	MARK	LUKE	JOHN
The genealogy of Jesus	1:1–17		3:23–38	
The birth of John the Baptist			1:5–25; 57–80	
The birth of Jesus	1:5–25; 2:1		2:1–20	
The wise men find Jesus	2:1–12			
The flight to Egypt	2:13–23			
The boy Jesus at the temple			2:41–50	
John the Baptist preaches and baptizes	3:1–12	1:1–8	3:1–20	
Jesus' baptism	3:13–17	1:9–11	3:21–22	
Jesus' temptation	4:1–11	1:12–13	4:1–13	
Jesus' first miracle at Cana				2:1–11
Jesus and Nicodemus				3:1–21
Jesus and the Samaritan woman				4:5–42
Jesus heals the nobleman's son				4:46–54
Jesus selects four disciples	4:18–22	1:16–20	5:1–11	
Demon-possessed man healed		1:23–28	4:31–37	
Jesus gives the Sermon on the Mount	5:1—7:29		6:20–49	
The parable of the two builders	7:24–27		6:47–49	
Jesus heals a leper	8:1–4	1:40–45	5:12–14	
The centurion's servant healed	8:5–13		7:1–10	
Peter's mother-in-law healed	8:14–15	1:29–31	4:38–39	
Life restored to the widow's son			7:11–17	
Jesus calms the storm	8:23–27	4:36–41	8:22–25	
Demon-possessed men healed	8:28–34	5:1–21	8:26–40	
Paralyzed man healed	9:1–8	2:3–12	5:18–26	
Life restored to Jairus' daughter	9:18–19, 23–26	5:22–24, 35–43	8:41–42, 49–56	
Woman healed of hemorrhage	9:20–22	5:25–34	8:43–48	
Blind man healed (Capernaum)	9:27–31			
Devil cast out of dumb man	9:32–34			

	Matthew	Mark	Luke	John
The disciples sent on tour	10:1—11:1	6:7–13	9:1–6	
Man with withered hand healed	12:9–14	3:1–5	6:6–11	
The parable of the sower	13:4–9, 18–23	4:1–20	8:14–15	
The parable of the tares	13:24–30			
The parable of the mustard seed	13:31–32	4:30–32	13:20–21	
The parable of the leaven	13:33–34			
The parable of hidden treasure	13:44			
The parable of the pearl	13:45			
The parable of the net	13:47–50			
John the Baptist killed	14:1–12	6:14–29	9:7–9	
The feeding of the 5,000	14:13–21	6:33–44	9:11–17	6:1–14
Jesus walks on the sea	14:22–33	6:45–52		6:15–21
Canaanite woman's daughter healed	15:21–28	7:24–30		
The feeding of the 4,000	15:32–38	8:1–9		
Blind man at Bethsaida healed		8:22–26		
Peter's great confession	16:13–26	8:27–37	9:18–25	
The transfiguration of Jesus	16:27—17:13	8:38—9:13	9:26–36	
Lunatic boy healed	17:14–21	9:14–29	9:37–43	
Tax money from fish's mouth	17:24–27			
The parable of the wealthy farmer			12:16–21	
Crippled woman healed			13:10–13	
The parable of the lost sheep	18:12–13		15:3–7	
The parable of the lost coin			15:8–10	
The parable of the prodigal son			15:11–32	
The parable of the unmerciful servant	18:23–35			
Jesus and the rich young ruler	19:16—20:16	10:17–31	18:18–30	
The adulterous woman				8:1–11
Man born blind healed				9:1–41
The parable of the good shepherd				10:1–18
The parable of the good Samaritan			10:30–37	
The parable of the friend at midnight			11:5–10	

Chart Continued on Following Page

	MATTHEW	MARK	LUKE	JOHN
The parable of the good father			11:11–13	
Lazarus raised from the dead				11:1–44
Jesus heals ten lepers			17:11–19	
The parable of the laborers in the vineyard	20:1–16			
Jesus heals the blind men	20:29–34	10:46–52	18:35–43	
Jesus and the barren fig tree	21:18–22	11:12–14, 20–26		
The parable of the man with two sons	21:28–32			
Jesus and Zacchaeus			19:1–10	
The parable of the landowner	21:33–44	12:1–9	20:9–19	
The triumphal entry of Jesus	21:1–11	11:1–10	19:29–40	12:12–19
Jesus clears the temple	21:12–13	11:15–19	19:45–48	
The parable of the marriage feast	22:1–14		14:16–24	
The parable of the fig tree	24:32	13:28–31	21:29–33	
The parable of the virgins	25:1–13			
The parable of the man, his servants, and the talents	25:14–30			
Jesus looks ahead to His crucifixion	26:1–5	14:1–2	22:1–2	
Mary anoints Jesus	26:6–13	14:3–9		12:2–8
Judas plots with authorities	26:14–16	14:10–11	22:3–6	
Last Passover and the Lord's Supper	26:20–29	14:17–21	22:7–30	
Jesus in Gethsemane	26:36–46	14:32–42	22:39–46	18:1
Betrayal and arrest of Jesus	26:47–56	14:43–52	22:47–53	18:2–12
Jesus' trial before Caiaphas and the Sanhedrin	26:57–68	14:55–65	22:63–65	18:24
Peter denies Jesus	26:69–75	14:66–72	22:54–62	18:15–18
Jesus' trial before Pilate	27:11–26	15:1–15	23:1–25	18:28–40; 19:1–15
The crucifixion of Jesus	27:33–56	15:22–41	23:33–49	19:16–30
The burial of Jesus	27:57–61	15:42–47	23:50–56	19:38–42
The resurrection of Jesus	28:1–10	16:1–7	24:1–12	20:1–10
Post-resurrection appearances	28:9–10, 16–20	16:9–18	24:13–48	20:11–29; 21:1–22
The ascension of Jesus		16:19–20	24:50–53	

THE PALESTINE OF JESUS' TIME

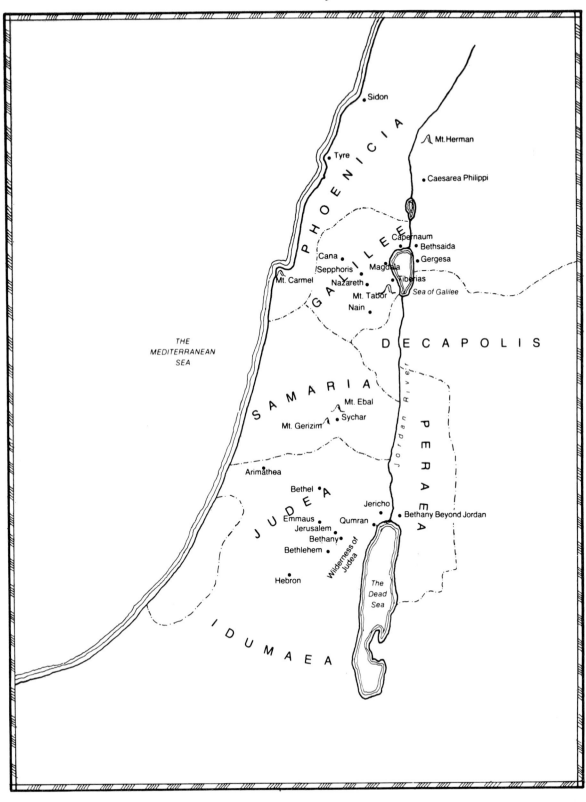

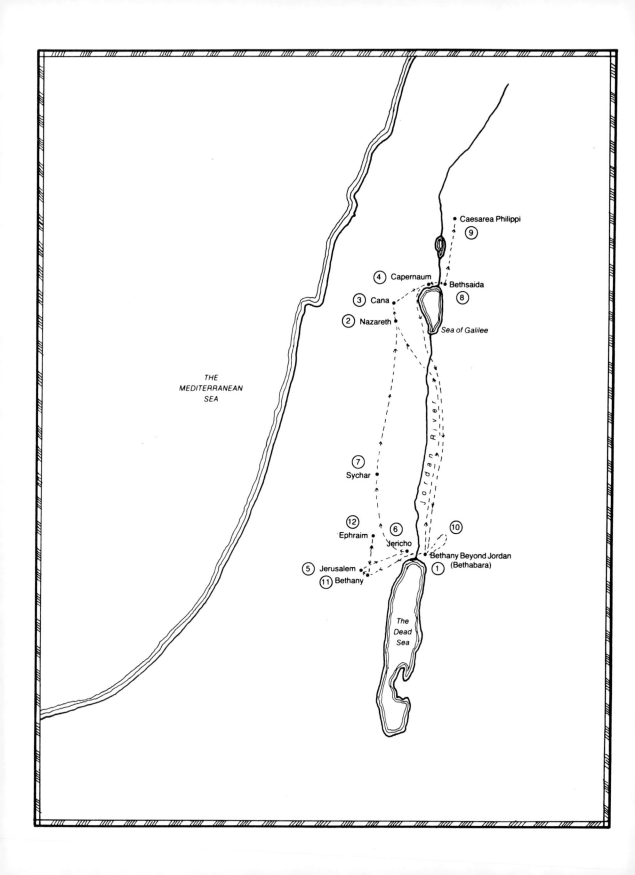

JESUS' TRAVELS IN THE GOSPEL OF JOHN

The Gospel of John places Jesus at the beginning of His ministry at Bethany Beyond Jordan ① but, undoubtedly, as Matthew and Mark indicate, Jesus had traveled there from Nazareth ② by taking the route just east of the Jordan River. Here Jesus was baptized by John the Baptist (John 1:19–34), but John does not give us the story of Jesus' temptation in the Judean wilderness. He does, however, give us the account of Jesus' first encounter with Andrew, Peter, Phillip, and Nathanael, who were early followers of John the Baptist (John 1:35–51).

From there Jesus traveled north and west to attend the wedding at Cana ③ just a few miles north of Nazareth ② (John 2:1–11). There, during the seven days of the wedding feast Jesus, in response to need, turned the water at the wedding feast into vintage wine. At the conclusion of the wedding feast Jesus traveled to Capernaum ④, a fishing town on the north shore of the Sea of Galilee (John 2:12).

Jesus heads south shortly on His Passover trip to Jerusalem ⑤ (John 2:13). And it was at this time, according to John, that He drove the money changers out of the temple and had His conversation with Nicodemus (John 2:14–3:21). And next we find Jesus and His disciples leaving Judea, possibly from Jericho ⑥, and heading northwest through Samaria where He had His meeting with the Samaritan woman at the Well of Jacob in Sychar ⑦ (John 4:5–38). They stayed on in Sychar for two days preaching and teaching; many of the Samaritans came to believe in Jesus during that time (John 4:39–42).

Upon leaving Sychar ⑦ they continued north through Nazareth ② to Cana ③. Word had apparently gotten around as far as Capernaum ④ that Jesus was in Cana ③ because we read that a Capernaum official, upon learning where Jesus was, found Him and begged Him to heal his son who was desperately ill at home. Jesus responded, not by going to Capernaum ④ at that moment, but by assuring him that his son was healed and would live (John 4:46–53).

In all probability Jesus later went on to Capernaum ④ but then He again traveled south, quite likely on either the route just west of the Jordan River, or the eastside route, to Jerusalem ⑤ where He healed the disabled man at the Pool of Bethesda (John 5:1–18).

John 6:1–15 has Jesus and His disciples back in Galilee, probably returning there from Jerusalem ⑤ by way of either the east or west route along the Jordan River. Out from Bethsaida ⑧ Jesus feeds the 5,000 with the five barley loaves and two fish.

From the region of Bethsaida ⑧ the disciples took a boat and traveled the short distance across the northern tip of the Sea of Galilee toward Capernaum ④. It was during this crossing that John tells us that Jesus appeared to the disciples while walking on the rough sea (John 6:16–21).

John 6:26–66 has Jesus teaching in the synagogue at Capernaum ④, after which, while the writer of John does not so indicate, they traveled north to Caesarea Philippi ⑨ where Peter gave his great confession of faith (John 6:67–71). Returning to Capernaum ④, Jesus stayed there until it was time for Him once again to head south to Jerusalem ⑤.

From John 7:1–10:39 Jesus is teaching and healing the sick in Jerusalem ⑤ and its environs. Then when the authorities attempted once again to kill Him, He retreated to an undefined region east of the Jordan River ⑩ (John 10:40–42) where he remained until He received word of Lazarus' death (John 11:1–6). Moving west across the Jordan River Jesus and His disciples made their way to Bethany ⑪ where he raised Lazarus from the dead (John 11:7–44).

The act of restoring life to Lazarus and the impact it had on the crowds polarized the Jewish authorities, and they determined that Jesus must die (John 11:45–53). It was this threat at the

Text Continues on Following Page

moment that caused Jesus to take His disciples to the secluded town of Ephraim ⑫, probably north of Bethany ⑪ some ten to fifteen miles (John 11:54).

Six days before the Passover they returned to Bethany ⑪ (John 12:1–11), and on what we know as Palm Sunday Jesus went to Jerusalem ⑤. From John 12:20–19:42 we have Jesus' actions and teachings through Holy Week, and His arrest and trial and crucifixion. In John 20:1–10 we read of Christ's resurrection, and from John 20:11–30 Jesus shows Himself to Mary in the garden and to His disciples, who said, "We have seen the Lord."

JERUSALEM/JERICHO ENVIRONS

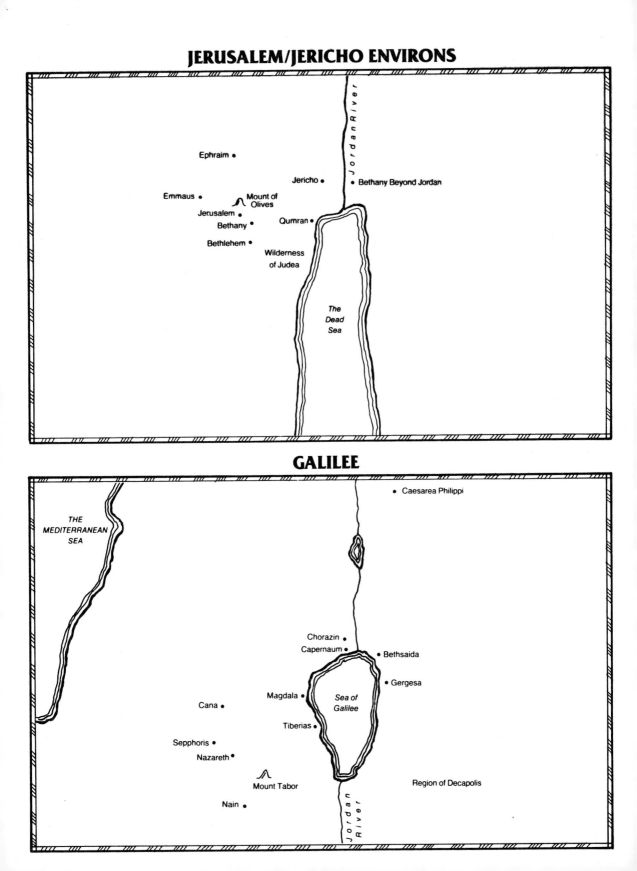

GALILEE